Bridport Arms.
to Beamister
Lane
Stake
STREET
to London
To Richd. Brodrepp of Mapperton Esqr.
Recorder of this Borough this PLAN,
is most Respectfully inscrib'd by
The Author.
Folly Mill
South East View of Bridport Church.
CALE
2 Furlongs
200
300
400
440 Yards or ¼ of a Mile

This book has been published
as a Limited Edition
of which this is

Number 264

A complete list of the
original subscribers is
printed at the back of
the book

THE BOOK OF BRIDPORT

FRONT COVER: Bridport in 1857. Probably the best-known picture of the town. (A photo-lithograph by J. Pouncy)

Ancient seal of Bridport; the oldest known design, 1374. (NR/B3/PQ34)

THE BOOK OF BRIDPORT

BY

BASIL SHORT & JOHN SALES

BARRACUDA BOOKS LIMITED
BUCKINGHAM, ENGLAND
MCMLXXX

PUBLISHED BY BARRACUDA BOOKS LIMITED
BUCKINGHAM, ENGLAND
AND PRINTED BY
FRANK ROOK LIMITED
TOWER BRIDGE ROAD
LONDON SE1

BOUND BY
BOOKBINDERS OF LONDON LIMITED
LONDON N5

JACKET PRINTED BY
CHENEY AND SONS LIMITED
BANBURY, ENGLAND

LITHOGRAPHY BY
SOUTH MIDLAND LITHOPLATES LIMITED
LUTON, ENGLAND

DISPLAY SET IN BASKERVILLE
& TEXT SET IN 12/14PT BASKERVILLE
BY BRIAN ROBINSON
NORTH MARSTON ENGLAND

ISBN 0 86023 079 1

Contents

Acknowledgements

The authors are grateful for the great deal of help they have received from a far larger number of people than it would be possible to name or, in some cases, even to recall. There are some, however, of whom special mention should be made, including the photographers who copied the work of others as well as contributing their own original work, namely Nancy Richards, Ron Frampton, Peter Payne and Michael Tattershall. Considerable use has been made of local records, particularly those of the old Bridport borough, deposited in the Dorset County Record Office in the care of Miss Holmes and her assistant archivists, and now the property of the successor bodies, West Dorset District Council and Bridport Town (Parish) Council. For these the catalogue references are given, B3 for the collection, the rest for the location within it. Acknowledgement of other sources is given by the following abbreviations.

BG	Bridport-Gundry Ltd
BM	Bridport Museum
BTC	Bridport Town Council
DCRO	Dorset County Record Office
DEE	*Dorset Evening Echo*
DM	Dorchester Museum
DMM	Dorset Military Museum
JH	John Hutchings
NR	Nancy Richards
PCC	St Mary's Parochial Church Council
PEP	Peter E. Payne
RF	Ron Frampton
SF	Society of Friends
MJT	Michael J. Tattershall
UC	Unitarian Chapel
UnCh	United Church

Burport

To Burport, which hath gained
That praise from every place, and worthilie obtained
Our cordage from her store, and cables should be made
Of any in that kind, most fit for marine trade.

Bert, whose batning mellowed banke
From all the British soyles, for hemp most hugelie rank
Doth bear away the best.

From *Polyolbion,* 1622
by Michael Drayton, Poet Laureate

Foreword

By Sir John Colfox, Bart.

It is indeed a pleasure and a privilege to be invited to write a Foreword to this book. My family has been directly concerned with the activities of Bridport almost continuously over the past 700 years, and I therefore welcome this tribute paid by Basil Short and John Sales, to a place and a community with a fascinating and honourable past.

Preface

By Miss Frances Reynolds, President of Bridport Civic Society and former Mayor of the Borough of Bridport.

People used to tell my father that he really ought to write a history of Bridport. Having lived here all his long life, he had a keen interest in, and considerable knowledge of its past, and was proud of its unique collection of local records. But, while he was always happy to talk or lecture on the subject, he never found time to write it all down, a fact that, until now, I have always regretted. He would have been the first to appreciate — as will so many — the enthusiasm, patience and skilful research that have gone in to the making of this book.

The text will appeal equally to the serious student and to the casual reader, and the careful selection of the many illustrations, with the clever reproduction from faded originals, adds immensely to the value of the volume.

Frances M. Reynolds.

Bridport has no History

This bald and unpromising statement appeared in Black's *Guide to Dorset,* published a little over a hundred years ago. At the time it seemed a proper thing to say, for not a great deal was known of the story of the town. There was, of course, a section in Hutchins' *History and Topography of the County of Dorset,* but this, in what is sometimes called the Bible of local history, is really something of a rag-bag of oddments, gathered from a variety of sources and put together with no obvious system of subject or chronology. In 1855 Rev Joseph Maskell, Assistant Curate of Allington and Walditch, managed to give *The History and Topography of Bridport* in one evening's lecture to the members of the Bridport Young Men's Institute; and he found it necessary to pad his subject out with an introduction about local history in general and then to begin with the story of the oolitic series of rocks! In fairness it must be said that not a great deal of information was available, and the few fragments of history, not all of them accurate, had to be supplemented with the fruits of a lively imagination.

Opportunity to improve this position came with the publication in 1877 of that part of the *Report of the Historical Manuscripts Commission* which dealt with manuscripts belonging to the Bridport Borough. Transcripts of many of the documents were made by Henry Thomas Riley. However, this was a government publication and, perhaps for that reason, it seems to have attracted little notice. Then, around the turn of the century, Thomas Wainwright made a thorough study of the Borough records and tried to promote interest by the publication of excerpts. This was extremely valuable work, but needed to be followed up, for, though Wainwright may be said to have *collected* the information for a history, there was still a need to *collate* it, that is, to see how the several records are related and when put together, may provide a more adequate picture of events than can be given by taking the individual manuscripts separately. It is only recently that this has been seriously attempted, and this book is one result. In expressing the hope that readers will be both instructed and delighted, we must add the further expectation that an even more adequate study will one day be attempted. Bridport *has* a history, but not all has yet been made available for telling.

What follows cannot be described as a history of the town, as there is still a great deal of material to be sifted and set in order. What we offer is a collection of highlights (and some shadows) in the town's story, a foretaste of an eventual definitive study.

Where it all Began

The general supposition has always been that the centre of Bridport was always where it is now — at the Town Hall, where East, West and South Streets meet. Thus it was assumed that the original settlement lay on an old east-west track, used by the Romans perhaps, and that the road to the south was really a sea-ward appendage. We ought perhaps to blame John Leland, the 16th century traveller, for that mistake, for he thought that the old chapel of St Andrew was the original parish church and that St Mary's church came later. We now realise that he was quite wrong.

A study of the map of Bridport in Hutchins' first edition (1774) will show that, although the easterly arm was then in process of being closed off, there was a cross-roads where St Mary's church stands. We can still walk the westward arm, which crosses the recreation ground and then goes uphill to Providence Cottage, where it joins Broad Street Lane and becomes a ridge way. But where does it go eastward? There are two main possibilities. Disciples of Alfred Watkins' *The Old Straight Track* will be intrigued by an alignment of Boarsbarrow Hill, near Loders, and Providence Cottage, with Thorncombe Beacon beyond, which does not quite pass through St Mary's church. This is not surprising, since the line of the east-west road goes along the north aisle of the present church, suggesting that there was a rebuilding at a fairly early date. Except for a stretch across the Asker plain, there is a fairly straight track still traceable most of the way, and walkable over a considerable part. An alternative, however, would be almost due east over the hill towards Shipton Gorge. An attractive aspect of this route is that it may represent a missing link in the Great Southern Ridgeway. To the north there are two routes converging on St Mary's church (certainly not on the Town Hall), one over the lee shoulder of Watton and Coneygar Hills and coming from the general direction of Beaminster, the other over the lee shoulder of Allington Hill to Dottery and then by Salway Ash to Buck's Head.

Where, then, does the road go to the south? We would suggest that it did not go very far. One topographical feature which is no longer very obvious (except when there is severe flooding) is the situation of the southern part of Bridport on a promontory between the two branches of an estuary. Borings taken on the glebe land to the west and south-west of St Mary's church show that at one time, probably not many centuries ago, the tide flowed up the valley on that side. The mud then laid down was followed by a layer of alluvium, suggesting that an interference with the tidal flow had changed the character of the flood plains. We have reason to believe that the valley on the east of the town, having become marshy, was recovered by drainage in the 12th or early 13th century, thus providing an area of land for hemp growing which was called Portmanfield. Before this happened, however, there must have been a landing place just south of the town, where the tide divided, and this would be one of the few safe landings in the Lyme Bay area. Thus the road south, though short, was perhaps important, and it is not surprising that a settlement should develop nearby.

There would, of course, need to be a causeway across the tidal stretch so that travellers could cross at low tide. There is at least one reference to a causeway, c1400 AD, and it would appear to refer to the westward one. We believe, on the evidence of a species count of the hedge on the south side of the path from the church to the recreation ground, that although the first part must be at least 1,500 years old, the causeway began at the bottom of Priory Lane and that reclamation of the adjoining land was made about the 16th century. This agrees with the statement in the charter by which Queen Elizabeth granted fairs and markets in 1593, that the outlet of the harbour of Bridport had recently been blocked by the sand of the sea.

According to the *Burghal hidage,* the catalogue of fortified towns compiled by Edward the Elder, son of Alfred the Great, there was in Dorset a town or *burh* named Bridian. Doubt has been expressed as to whether this could be identified with Bridport, and another location has been suggested. However, other evidence must be considered. In the first place we know that the northern boundary of the historic borough, the Town Ditch, called in earlier times La Wydych (the wide ditch) or, along the eastern part, the muridge, ran along Rax Lane and was then displaced a little to the north to continue behind the other East Street properties, (see Hutchins' map). Recently we observed that there was another Town Ditch to the south of East Street and not quite parallel with it, running behind the properties on the south side of the street. This, at first sight, might seem to confirm the traditional idea that the town was based upon the east-west main route (now the A35). There are two main reasons for rejecting this. In the first place the line of this second ditch, especially when extended westwards, suggests that it is protecting something to the south of it, being concave in that direction. Secondly (and, we think, decisively) there are properties in South Street and to the north of this ditch which, in mediaeval times, were described as being 'without the bars'. This would imply that a gate just north of the present Museum was the *northern* gate at an early stage of development, and this agrees with our belief that the original settlement lay in the vicinity of St Mary's church.

The northern ditch of this Saxon town which, according to Domesday Book, contained 120 houses in Edward the Confessor's time, would appear to run from King Street on the east to St Michael's Lane on the west, then running due south from these extremities to south of the parish church, perhaps as far south as Bolton Place, where there is what appears to be a portion of bank. There is also a bank behind Prospect Place in King Street. However, this would give a town larger than we would have expected, Bridian being based upon 760 hides of land, representing a wall length of 3,135 feet. This might be explained by the nature of the eastern and western boundaries which, being marshy and tidal over most of their length, might not require a ditch and bank. Alternatively, the *burh,* as first constructed, may have been smaller, and we can plot a smaller town, based on existing features, which would require the prescribed wall length. This may have been enlarged later, both to contain more land and to provide a more defensible line, nearer to the rivers. It is, of course, possible that, as a defensive enclosure on a promontory (cf. Christchurch and Wareham), its main defence was a ditch and bank separating the promontory from the mainland, with a similar system overlooking the vulnerable landing place at the south end. The number of hides would then be more significant of the size of the garrison than of the length of the wall.

Whatever the topographical situation it seems clear that the military location soon became important as a market or port, administered by a portreeve. It is probable that many of the 120 houses were built in the period from Athelstan to Edward the Confessor, as the town grew in commercial rather than military importance. As a borough, Bridport had a mint, coins existing from the time of Ethelred II. Yet apparently it suffered some decline, so that at the time of the Domesday survey there were only 100 houses, the other 20 being in ruins, and the inhabitants were too poor to pay their taxes.

In Ponchesford Lane. The authors with other members of the Civic Society committee. Dorothy Wood, Jim Chaplin and Frances Sanctuary, looking at the hedge to the west of St Mary's church. Probably the town's oldest above-ground feature. (PEP/DEE)

ABOVE: An early photograph (1859) from the tower of the parish church, looking north along South Street. (BM) BELOW: A more recent photograph (1970) of the same view. In both pictures the widening of the street in the foreground suggests the position of the Saxon market-place. (RF/BM)

The Burh

The depressing picture of the town given by Domesday seems to have changed considerably by the mid-13th century. So has the character of the town itself. Unfortunately we lack documentary evidence in the borough archives for the early part of the century, the earliest dated manuscript being of the year 1240. Very few are likely to be older, and then only by a year or two. That fact in itself, however, suggests that the new growth was quite recent and that the town was just establishing itself as a well-organised community.

On the other hand there is evidence of growth at a rather earlier period. There is evidence from the Rolls of the Royal Exchequer that in 1211 a considerable amount of cordage and sailcloth was being produced and that net-making was being carried on. Then, in 1213 King John gave an order to the town to produce as much rope of different kinds and cordage for ballistae as was physically possible, asking the ropers to work 'night and day'. It is also evident that, as in other places, population pressure had made it necessary to make more land available. It would appear that the flat land to the east of the town, once estuarial but having become marshy, had been reclaimed by draining to produce quite a large area of land for hemp growing. Its name, Portmanfield, suggests that there was an element of communal enterprise. It seems that the growth of the town took place in definite stages. Probably the first extension was by the addition of a rectangular area immediately to the north of the earlier town's northern ditch, thus moving the boundary to the line of Rax Lane. That the town did not then extend to the West Bridge is suggested by a deed in which a property in West Street is described as *extra barros* (outside the gates). These gates were probably near the top of St Michael's Lane. The extension to the East Bridge was made wider from north to south; hence the irregular shape of the northern boundary.

There are a great many property deeds of the 13th and early-14th centuries, and these, apart from a few relating to the manors of Allington, Walditch, Shipton and Bradpole, are of properties in the northern extension of the town. It looks as though an entirely new community was establishing itself. Moreover the majority of the names appear to be of Norman origin, and even those who have English names (of local manors, for instance) seem in many cases to be originally Norman. In one or two cases we can see the changes that took place. So de Sermunville becomes de Sturthill, Gervase becomes de Bridport and later de Chideock. Cristina de Stikelane was probably a member of the Quarel family and related to the Killings and Talles.

Otherwise names like Bonvile, Corbyn, Clopet, Coterel, Criket, Mankeville, Marais, de Morville, Maudit, de Normanville, Percy, Rousel and Tracy reveal a Norman origin, while many others look more like corruptions of French and Norman names than originally English ones.

One explanation of this is that there was in this period a general migration into the towns, which expanded as a result. People came in from the rural manors, many holders of these manors finding it advantageous to acquire urban burgages. Many rural landlords were of Norman origin so we can in fact identify some of the manors from which the new people came. There is, however, another explanation to account for some of the newcomers. When King John lost Normandy in 1204, many of his subjects living there felt obliged to leave their homes and come to England, some out of loyalty perhaps and some by expulsion. Of one notable case we know — Thomas de Gorges, who was deprived of his castle and, though very much later, was made warden of the royal castle of Powerstock.

Not only was Dorset one of the nearest English counties, but it had some affinities with Normandy. Climate and geology are similar and it is possible (though not much is known about the Norman aspect at that time) that there were similarities in agriculture and craft — hemp and flax growing, rope and sailcloth making. In other words the Bridport area would be a convenient first stop for the migrants. This could cast a new light upon King John's order for rope. He may have thought it useful to have an enlarged pool of labour and wise not to let problems arise from hands insufficiently occupied.

We suggest that the northern part of the town, based upon a new east-west road, was virtually a new town, different in several respects from the old one, but mainly in ethnic origin. This looks like a recipe for conflict and, as we shall see, it bore its own peculiar consequence.

One of Bridport's historical puzzles arises from the fact that it has two sites each with 'The Castle' as one of its traditional titles. Was there ever a castle attached to the town? Does the confusion arise because there have been two main guesses as to its location? Or is it possible that there were, perhaps at different times, two castles?

The sites are: (1) that of the museum, at the top of South Street, its position, just inside the gate of the Saxon *burh,* suggesting at first that it had some relation to that town; and (2) the Chantry, or Dungeness, or the Priest's House, at the bottom of South Street, which we once thought might possibly have served the same function as the one in the north, so that we guessed at the position of the southern ditch of the *burh* by the analogy. However, there is another possibility.

The location of the northern castle suggests that, though it may not have existed in the early days of the *burh,* it was probably built while the limits of the town were still defined by the Saxon defences. During the civil war between Stephen and Matilda, the town was captured (1150) by Henry Plantagenet, who received the submission of the castellan. It is known that a great many castles were built by the protagonists during that war, and that when Henry came to the throne, he had most of these castles razed to the ground. This may explain why, in the 13th century, the site was referred to either as the Castle or as Castlehay, ie theground where a castle had been. The site is quite small and almost square, having been taken out of a larger plot called Morterhay. The castle was probably a typical square keep or donjon, purpose-built to serve the crisis and enjoying only a short life. Perhaps the name of the surrounding site, Morterhay (field of the dead?), implies that the engagement in which Henry captured the castle was particularly hard-fought.

We believe that the southern site was outside the bounds of the Saxon town and overlooked the vulnerable landing place by the confluence of the two rivers. An occasion for the building of this suggests itself, if we accept the idea that the new town arose partly from direct immigration from Normandy. After King John's defeat there the Pope was encouraging King Philip of France to invade England. That some preparations were made to resist him is to be expected; a new castle was built in Guernsey, for example. Some of Bridport's inhabitants had more than one reason to defend themselves, and it is possible that they built another keep at the point of greatest danger. The need soon diminished and the building could be adapted for other uses. The Chantry may well have begun life as an early 13th century castle. Certainly architects have been known to declare that the building has Norman characteristics.

However, it is only fair to add that the building is so confusing, mainly because of the many alterations it has undergone, that every expert who visits it seems to come to a different opinion. So we must allow the possibility, difficult though it is to reconcile with the documents, that the building is much later, the original castle on the site having disappeared, to be replaced by a composite structure, part house and part chapel. We could make it roughly contemporary with the parish church, and perhaps suggest that it was then that the castle was built. After all, the French were being a bit of a nuisance early in the 15th century. But what we do about St Katherine's chantry of the mid-14th century it is difficult to see. Let us admit that there are still some mysteries, even in solid stone.

Whatever the truth about Bridport's 'Castles', Bridport was a market town in Saxon times. The creation of the *burh* provided a protected position in which a market place could be established and where merchants could settle. The building line of South Street probably goes back to this period and suggests that the first market was in the main street just north of the cross-roads. Its centre would be before the present Woodman inn.

The new town of the 13th century had its own centre and drew trade away from the old one to the place where South Street met the new east-west road. This would have been quite spacious until the White Friars were allowed to build their oratory and priory there, thus creating the still rather restricted access into South Street.

Records relating to the market go back at least to the late 14th century, those of the 'pie-powder' courts beginning in 1438. (These were courts of summary jurisdiction sitting on market days, named from the old French 'piedspoudreux', the dusty-footed ones.) From the records we know that leases were granted for shambles — covered stalls — which stood not only in the position shown on Hutchins' map, these being the main butchers' stalls, but also down South Street, among them the shoe shambles, which lay between the Swan and the flesh shambles. Matters of weight and quality were also controlled. Leather had to be certified and sealed, bread and beer had to be 'good and wholesome for man's body', weights and measures of length had to be true. Inspectors were appointed at the annual Law Day when the bailiffs and other officers were elected. The market was used by merchants living both in and outside the borough, but there were attempts made to restrict outside competition. Thus, towards the end of the 16th century, the local bakers asked the court to forbid country bakers from selling bread in the town.

When Queen Elizabeth I made her new grant of fairs and markets in 1594, an extra market day was added to the customary 'Satterdaies Markett' and the right to sell sheep and cattle was granted. This led to an enlargement of the market and no doubt added to the congestion on the streets. This congestion became quite serious in the 18th century, particularly with an increase of traffic on the 'great western road'. Eventually, stimulated by a fire at the Guildhall in 1782, the Corporation decided to act. A Bill was presented to Parliament to enable the building of a market house and the removal of the shambles and other obstructions in the High Street. The result was the opening in 1786 of the Market House, now known as the Town Hall, its 37 butchers' stalls, accommodated in the ground floor, being later replaced by one butcher's shop and the public conveniences.

Cattle and sheep were penned and sold in the streets; but off-street selling was encouraged and several sites were used. One was near West Mill, another on West Street (next to the present Post Office), and more recently the market was in St Michael's Lane. Other stalls were still allowed in the streets, the number varying from time to time. There has been, for instance, a considerable increase during the last few years, the stalls selling greengroceries, fish, flowers and plants, clothes, haberdashery, pottery, tools, all manner of fancy goods, antiques, bric-a-brac, etc. The present buyers and sellers may not realise how ancient is the tradition which they continue.

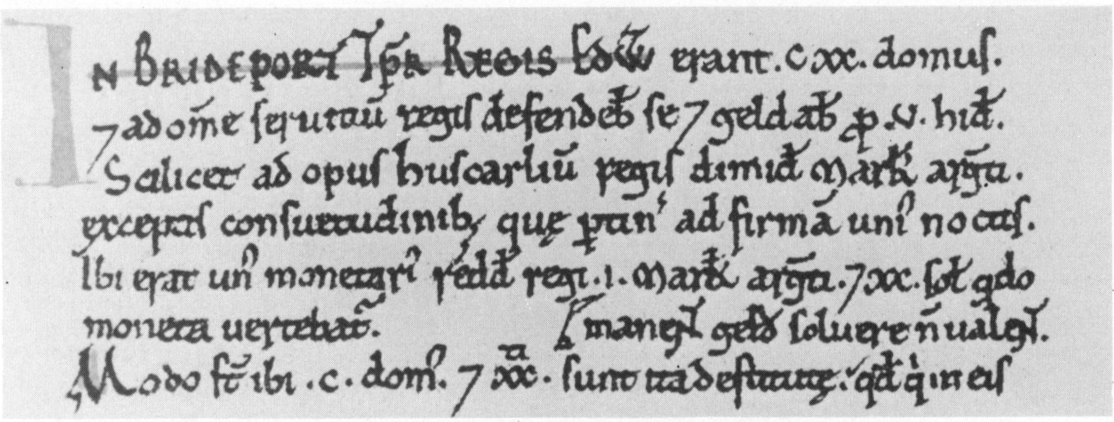
IN BRIDEPORT TPR REGIS EDW erant .c.xx. domus.
7 ad omne servitium regis defendeb se 7 geldab p .v. hid.
Scilicet ad opus huscarliu regis dimid mark argti.
exceptis consuetudinib que ptin ad firma uni noctis.
Ibi erat un monetari redd regi .i. mark argti 7 xx. sol qdo
moneta uertebat. manent geld soluere n ualent.
Modo st ibi .c. dom 7 xx. sunt ita destitute qd q in eis

Bridport's main entry in Domesday. The 120 houses in King Edward's time had been reduced to 100 by 1086. (NR/DCRO)

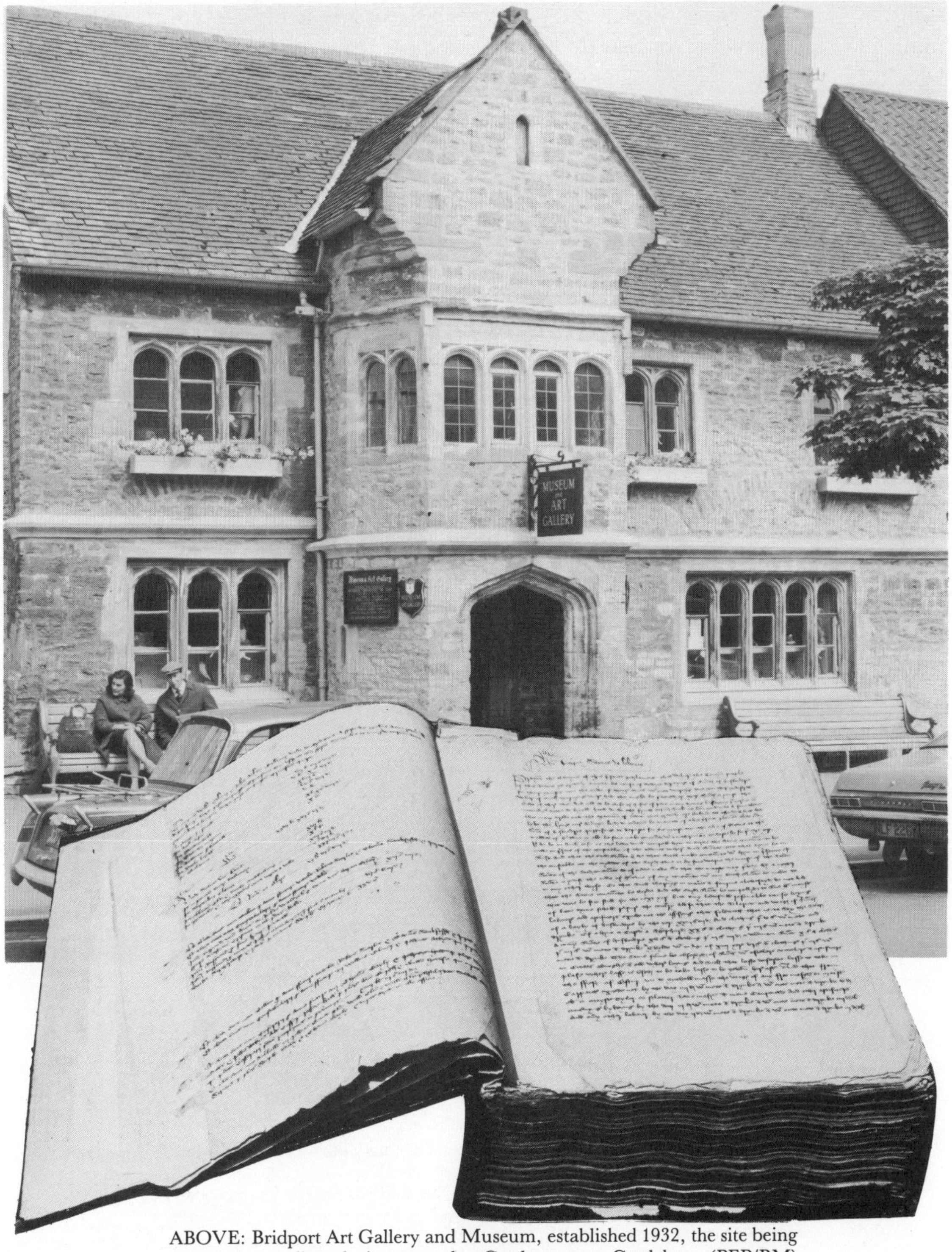

ABOVE: Bridport Art Gallery and Museum, established 1932, the site being known in mediaeval times as the Castle, or as Castlehay. (PEP/BM)
BELOW: The 'Red Book called Domesday', records the corporation's activities from 1444 to 1817, except for the Civil War and Commonwealth.

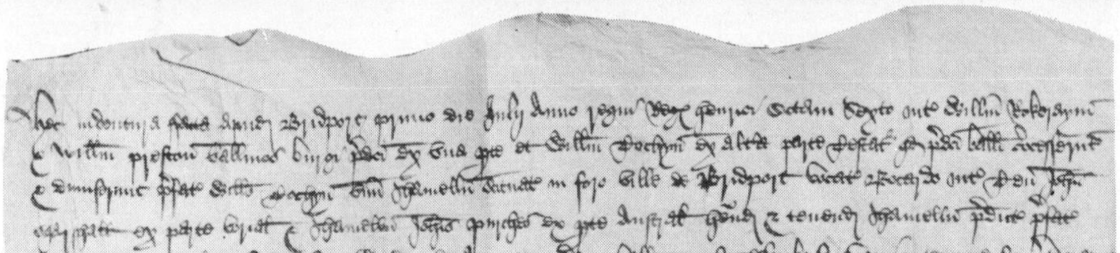

ABOVE: The Chantry, from a painting by Gulielma Stephens in 1870, when Castle Square was being built. (NR/BM) INSET: The Chantry, South Street. (BM) BELOW: The Bridport market had shambles (covered stalls, not necessarily for meat) both opposite St Andrew's chapel in East Street and in South Street. One location was called 'Bocardo', as in this lease, or 'Buccadoes Lane'. The passage between the Town Hall and the Greyhound is still known to local people as 'Bucky Doo', thus preserving a name as old as this deed of 1514. (NR/B3/021)

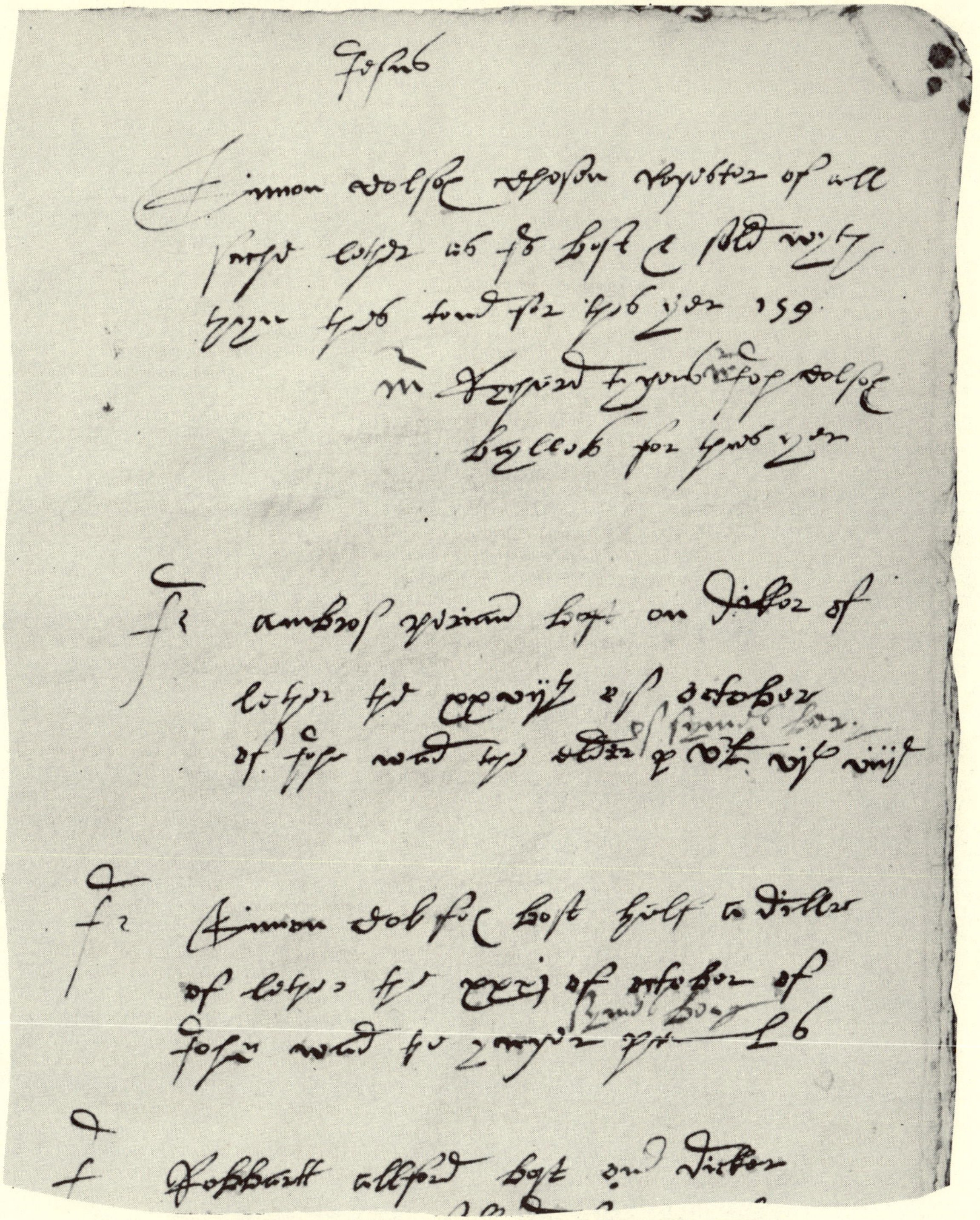

Part of the first page of the record kept by Simon Colfox in 1590 when he was searcher and sealer of leather for the Bridport market. It shows who bought how many hides from whom, eg: Ambros Periam bought one diller (ten hides) on 27 October of John Wade the elder of Symondsbury, for £5 6s 8d. Notice the pious invocation 'Jesus' with which the document begins. (NR/B3/01)

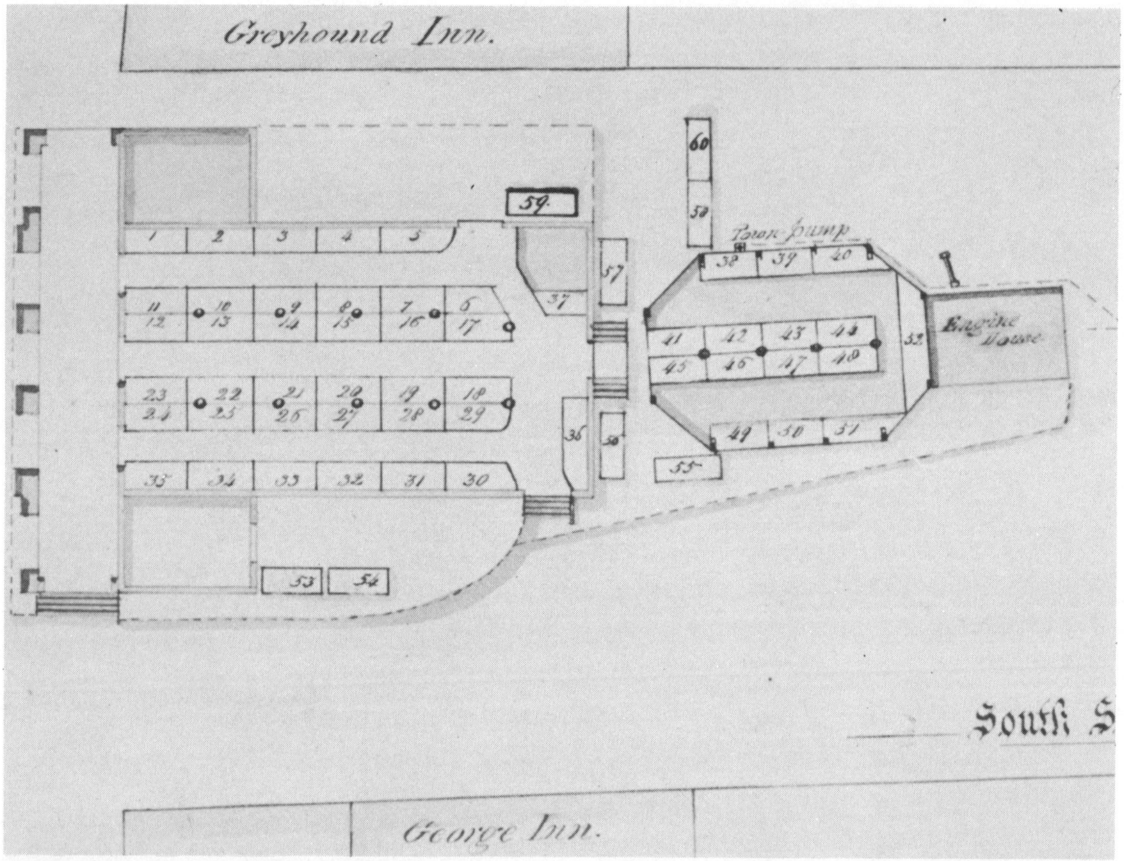

ABOVE: The new Market House, opened in 1786, having 37 butchers' stalls on the ground floor, the town hall being above. To the rear was a smaller building, now demolished, then used as a corn and general market. (NR/B3/047) BELOW: The old cattle market in Victoria Grove, upon which site the Post Office was built, obliging the auctioneers, Messrs W. Morey & Sons, to find a new site. (BM)

ABOVE: In 1902 the cattle market returned to West Street, pending the creation of the new market in St Michael's Lane. (E.C. Hare/BM) LEFT: Another view of the street market. Note the play-bills in the background. (BM) RIGHT: Bridport market c1913; Samuel Clent, butcher, (with umbrella) bargaining with Edward Smith, farmer of Stoke Abbot, the subject being lambs. (BM)

St Mary's Church in 1859, before it was extended to the west. (MT/PCC)

A Plain Substantial Structure

The origins of the parish church of St Mary, in South Street, are not known, but probably belong to an early period. The cross-roads by which it was built suggests that the foundation is older than that of the chapel of St Andrew c1261. It is probable that the earliest building was Saxon and on a site slightly to the south of the present one, which lies partly over the line of the east-west road. As to the date of the present building there has been some disagreement. It is generally claimed that the oldest part is of the 13th century and some ground-level stonework even older. Joseph Maskell, curate of Allington and Walditch, said in 1855, having discussed the style at some length: 'Its date therefore may be safely fixed about AD1400'. What is interesting about this is that, although Maskell appears to have no knowledge of the borough records, they partially support his conjecture. Adam Bouleghe, apparently a master-mason and a member of the gild of St Mary and St James, was paid 40s, a considerable sum, for work on the church in 1401. At or just after Easter, 1404, both the bishop and his suffragan were here for the 'celebration' of the church, and this was clearly a special occasion, for later in the account we find the entries: 'Paid the Lord Bishop of Salisbury for the dedication of the church, £4 13s 4d. In wine 3s 3½d'. Just before these are the entries: 'For 17 waggons for carrying to the causeway, 11s 1d. For men hired to carry stone and earth from the churchyard to make the causeway, 2s 2d. For one rammer bought for laying the stones, 1d'. This suggests a great deal of rubble from a demolished building was removed and used in the repair of the tide-washed causeway to the west of the town.

The records also tell of work done on the church and bell-tower in 1406, the superintendent of work on the tower being Nicholas Portlond. Perhaps this refers to the building of the present tower.

Alterations were made from time to time. Thus in 1628 a gallery was built over St Katherine's aisle by Henry Waade of Topsham, who asked that profits from the sale of sittings should be used to buy bread for the aged poor. Galleries were also erected in the 18th century and, with other things, earned the disapproval of Joseph Maskell. He described the church in 1855 as a 'plain substantial structure' yet with 'beauties of its own, and I would particularly ask you to notice the very unusual double chancel, a chancel with north and south aisles, where doubtless before the Reformation were three gorgeous altars, each of them crowded with willing worshippers and covered with gifts. The clustered columns which support the tower are very fine'. It did not all please him, however. 'The west end of the church is completely barbarised and disfigured. In fact the whole church must have suffered much since the decay of architectural taste, and it is manifest that so long as it is filled with those unsightly pews and galleries, its beauty will always be disfigured. The style of pew that prevails in Bridport seems to me a cross between a horse-box and an Irish car'. A few years later, in 1860, changes were made, some of which would certainly have pleased him. The nave was lengthened and the west door restored, the galleries removed and the pews changed. He might not be happy, however, about the loss of part of the chancel, now occupied by the organ and the clergy vestry, but once the chantry of (probably) St Nicholas.

Hutchins gives a list of the rectors of the church, with their patrons, beginning with Peter de Colyngton in 1317. We have found two earlier than this. One was Hosbert, or Osbert, a witness to two of many deeds of gift to St John's hospital in the 13th century, one dated 1265. The other was John, one of the executors of Master John de Bridport, who is mentioned in a royal writ of 1306. Hutchins does not list the great number of chaplains associated with the church when it contained several chantries. Several wills in the late 14th and early 15th centuries record bequests to nearly a dozen clergy, many of them directly associated with the church. Moreover, in the case of the parish gild of the Torches, the list of members in 1421 is headed by John Helyer, the rector, and three chaplains, John Mustard, John Bexington and Robert Gylys.

One of the most complete lists is given on a document of 1446 relating to Indulgences for those contributing to the repair of Bridport harbour. Here are John Helyer, the rector, Francis Cotys, chaplain of St Katherine, William Aunger, chaplain of the Blessed Virgin, and John Bonamy, chaplain of St Nicholas (these being the three chantries in the parish church), then John Shipper, prior of St John's, William Whittock and John Trewyne, chaplains of the Munden chantry, John Hasard, prior of St Mary Magdalene, and Robert Brode, stipendiary chaplain there.

A curious feature of this is that it comes a few years after the rector had been at the centre of a local dispute, leading the bishop to hold an inquiry under Canon John Druitt, who had summoned the rector to appear before him, but without response. He therefore proceeded to hear the complaint of a large body of parishioners that the rector had refused to maintain a chaplain at St Andrew's and to allow the chaplain of St Katharine to celebrate Mass according to ancient custom.

The registers begin on 10 April 1600 with the burial of Christopher Terrent. The churchwarden's books begin in 1762 and give full lists of ratepayers. A recent book comments upon the strange position of the parish church, 'so far from the centre of the town'. This reference is only topographical. The parish church has played a part at the centre of the life of the town for many centuries.

ABOVE LEFT: St Mary's Church: interior prior to the restoration of 1860. (NR/BM) RIGHT: South porch and window of parvise chamber. (BM) BELOW: Interior after restoration. (NR/BM)

ABOVE: The Unitarian Chapel, East Street (1794). (UC) BELOW: The former Wesleyan Chapel (1838), now the Bridport Arts Centre. (UnCh)

ABOVE: The Baptist Chapel, Chard's Mead (1841). INSET: The Congregational Church (1860), now the United Church. (BM) BELOW LEFT: St Swithin's Church, Allington (1826). (BM) RIGHT: The Catholic Church of St Mary and St Catherine (1978) in Victoria Grove. (PEP/BM)

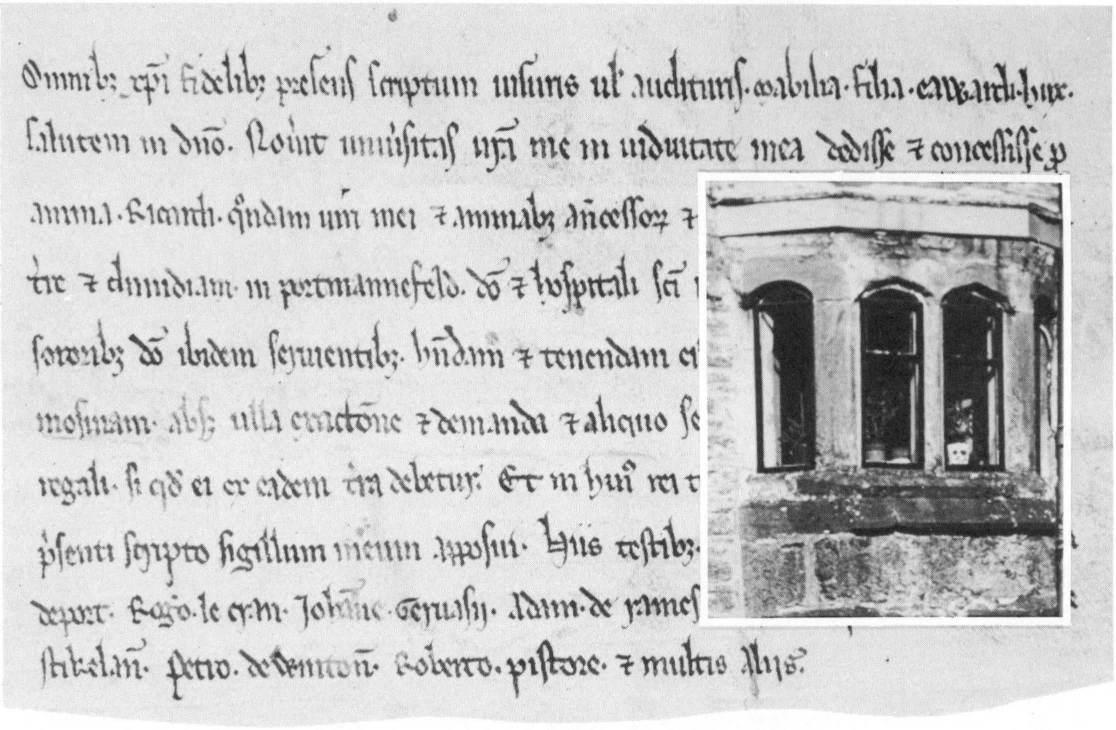

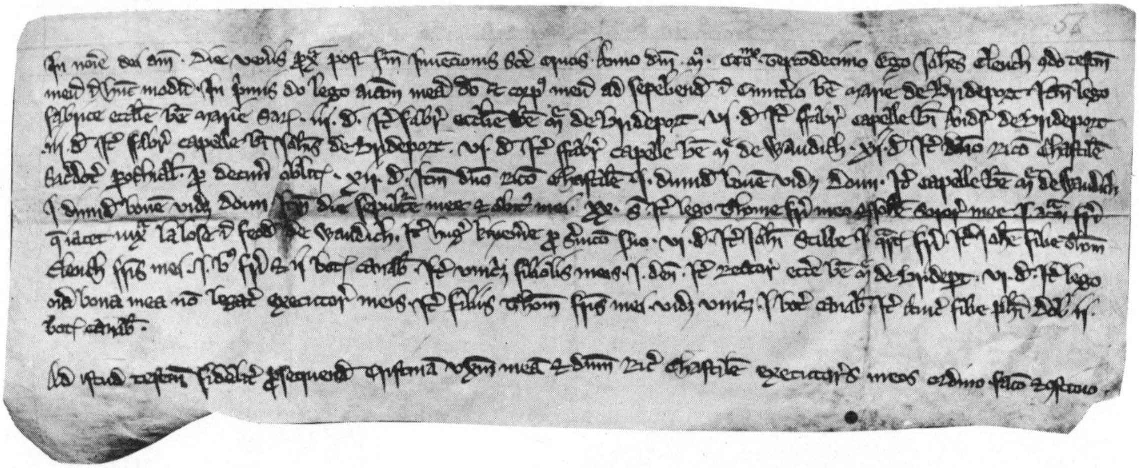

ABOVE: A mid-13th century deed recording a grant to St John's priory and hospital 'and the brethren and sisters there serving God'. The wording of the deed suggests that it may be a grant by his daughter, Mabilia, adding to the foundation gift of Edward Hux. (NR/B3/CD69) INSET: The oriel window of St John's priory and hospital. (BM) BELOW: The oldest extant will. The oldest will used to be that of Cristina de Stikelane (1268) but it has been lost. We must now be content with that of John Clench (1313), not strictly of Bridport, but of Walditch. (NR/B3/Y1)

Praising God

A development which seems to have accompanied the establishing of the new town was the appearance of a religious community at its eastern end. When it first appeared it probably lay outside the town, which then grew towards it. This was the hospital and priory of St John the Baptist. (John Leland confused the issue by making it appear that the hospital was at one end of the town and the priory at the other, one of several of his mistakes.) There are a number of deeds relating to this foundation and they all speak of the priory and hospital at the East Bridge 'and the brethren and sisters there praising God'. In other words it was a double order. We cannot relate it directly to any of the known double orders, though its pattern may have been suggested by the Norman Abbey of Fontevrault. However there was a similar foundation at Ilchester with a similar dedication, founded about 1220.

Presumably the priory had a lay founder-patron but, although there are many deeds of gift, there is none which could be identified as a foundation deed. By these gifts the institution must have become wealthy, possessing most of Portmanfield as well as lands in Shipton and Walditch, taking the profits of Killing's Mill (later called Folly Mill) and probably of the East Mill beyond the bridge, and having several properties in the town.

Apart from these deeds there is a great deal of information about the hospital and priory. We know the names of some of the early priors, from William in the late 13th century, followed by Roger de Rydeclive, Master John de Bridport and Richard Castelayn. There is a little information in an inventory of goods made in 1453, when the Bailiffs of the borough handed over to John Syltere, the new prior, the 'implements' of the priory which they had received from the former prior, Hugh. The rooms mentioned were the Chapel, Hall, Pantry, Kitchen and Chamber. From the list it is difficult to suppose that many guests or sick could be accommodated; nor is there any reference to rooms for the 'brethren and sisters', who probably occupied bare cells.

The last prior was John Chard, who was pensioned when the priory was dissolved, the property passing to Nicholas Prideaux and others.

For a long time St John's seems to have been a private residence, but in 1769 it was rebuilt and opened as The Marquis of Granby, a coaching inn to cater for travellers on the 'great western road'. When the inn closed in the 19th century it became a factory for making leather shoe uppers, the Granby Works. It is now the Masonic Hall.

There is some mystery attached to the origin of the chapel and priory of St Michael, though we have far more information about its daily life than we have about St John's. That, like St John's, it catered for travellers and visitors to the town is apparent from the accounts.

It has often been stated that the chapel was founded in 1321 by Robert de Faryndon. Yet, according to a deed of 1279, the chapel of St Michael existed then in West Street. Moreover one of the bequests of Cristina de Stikelane was to this chapel.

We know the position of the chapel. It was on the corner of West Street and St Michael's Lane, on the west of that lane, and some of its stonework was still visible there in the middle of last century. The position of other buildings is less certain, though there is a tradition which locates a priory further south, near the beginning of Priory Lane. Perhaps the two were connected. That St Michael's Priory had extensive grounds, including a garden and an orchard, is suggested by the accounts.

It is possible to link this mystery with another. Cristina de Stikelane left money to several Franciscan priories, one of which is unnamed (as indeed is the location of the Carmelite priory). The chapel and priory of St Michael could originally have been a Franciscan foundation, which fell into disuse and was restored as a chantry by Robert de Faryndon. It is interesting that Priory Lane appears in at least one mediaeval deed as 'Friern Lane'.

The gift of Robert de Faryndon is recorded in a deed of 18 January 1321, and one of the witnesses was Thomas Bonville. It is appropriate that part of the chapel site is now occupied by Bonfield's Garage, the Norman name having undergone a slight change. The gift was to provide the means whereby the chaplain, Nicholas Michel, could celebrate a daily mass for the souls of Robert and his wife, Johanna.

In 1361 the foundation was enlarged, John de Munden providing the means for another altar and chaplain, so that St Michael's became a double chantry. Two chaplains were appointed, Nicholas Gurtopp and Nicholas de Portland. Only the latter was a new appointment, for Nicholas Gurtopp had been in the town at least as early as 1342. He may have been Nicholas Michel's successor or, of course, he could have been the same person, there being no stability of surnames then.

Full accounts exist of the income of the priory and, in even greater detail, of the expenditure. These have been described in K. L. Wood Legh's *A Small Household of the Fifteenth Century,* and by Thomas Wainwright in *The Bridport Borough Records and Ancient Manuscripts.* The accounts (for 1453-60) tell of the diet of the chaplains and their guests, rather restricted by our standards but probably good for their time; about the maintenance of the buildings and grounds and the various properties from which the income was drawn; and about the guests who were given temporary lodging. One of the chaplains, William de Savernake, was the accountant, but his excellent example was not followed by his colleague, John Trewyn, nor by any others.

At the dissolution the property was allocated to Nicholas Prideaux and William Morris. The last incumbents were John Mayne and John Baker.

The Friars, Black, Grey and White, were an interesting phenomenon of the 13th century. At first they seemed like a breath of fresh air in the religious life of the country—young men, unattached to the parish establishment, committed to preaching and poverty, devoted to the faith, in some areas providing a striking contrast with those parish clergy who were indifferent, ignorant, incontinent and self-seeking. Not surprisingly they had popular appeal, and many people were drawn away to receive mass from and confess to these mendicant preachers, to the dismay of bishops and parochial clergy.

Two of the orders were represented in Bridport. The Franciscans were here, though we can find no evidence to tell us just what they did or where they worked. In the case of the Carmelites, or White Friars, the situation is different: there is abundant evidence of their work and of their location. Some of that evidence exists because of the difficulties they had to face.

There is a hint of problems in a letter, believed to be from Cardinal Ottoboni, who was Papal Legate from 1265-68, in which he asked the Bishop of Salisbury 'to permit the friars to perform divine office without molestation or difficulty in the oratory which they have built at Bridport'. Evidence of the location of this oratory is provided by Bridport's oldest Will, that of the Lady Cristina de Stikelane. She was probably a member of the Norman family of Quárel (Carel), which held lands in the Winterborne valley. She took her name from the part of the road from Blandford to Milton which crossed that valley by a steep path (a stikel lane), and her family had taken part in that migration which brought people to the town from their rural manors. Cristina, in her will, was generous to many churches and to many religious orders, but she treated one church and one order with particular favour. The church was the chapel of St Andrew, built on the site now occupied by the Town Hall and, according to a deed of that year, newly established in 1267. The order was that of the Friars of Mount Carmel. It is reasonable to assume that the Carmelite oratory, built by the Friars, was the Chapel of St Andrew.

Equally the three clergy who were witnesses of Cristina's w ill were almost certainly members of the order. They were Adam the Chaplain (presumably of St Andrew's), Richard Robe, his second name probably a sobriquet earned by his white cloak, and Clement de Eysse, a member of a local family, from the manor of Ash, a few miles to the north of the town.

These men probably built the chapel, with some local help.

Its position at the centre of the new town, analogous to the position of St Mary's in the old town, gave it a status which the new citizens acknowledged but which was probably offensive to the rector and to the Bishop of Salisbury. In a gift by Bartholomew, son of Cristina, to the Mass of St Mary in St Andrew's chapel, he says that 'no one of the rectors, fermors or chaplains of the church of St Mary in the same vill shall intermeddle therewith'. It seems that the Bishop, in order to put pressure on the wealthy lay-people who supported the Friars, had threatened to deny them the use of the ecclesiastical courts. This would be a serious matter, for testamentary matters, all that was involved in the proving of wills, required confirmation in those courts and were recorded by them. The answer of the citizens was that they would, through their magistrates and their own local courts, do this for themselves. Thus we find that such legal matters, from about this time, were dealt with locally, an unusual situation found in few other places.

Reference to the Mass of St Mary leads us to a peculiarity of the Carmelites and to another problem. The Carmelite Friars were particularly devoted to the Blessed Virgin, having seven feasts in her honour, over and above the customary ones. It is not surprising that they had an altar within their chapel of St Andrew, dedicated to St Mary, and a society of worshippers to support it—the members of the Mass of St Mary. It may not always be clear, when St Mary is mentioned in a deed, whether the reference is to the parish church or to the chapel within St Andrew's. The references at this time were usually to the latter, being either to the Mass or to the Chantry of St Mary, and being supported by those people in the northern part of the town who looked upon St Andrew's chapel as their spiritual home. There were a great many benefactions to the Mass and many leases of property belonging to it. It was certainly a prosperous institution, devoted no doubt to prayers for the dead; but we have no evidence of other functions. There was also another society, the fraternity or gild of the Holy Trinity. This also had property, and was probably the merchants' gild, thus playing an important part in the administration of the town.

A few years ago we made a curious discovery—that there still exists a picture of the chapel, or at least of its tower shortly before it was demolished in 1785. The picture is too small for any detail, but it suggests that the style was Romanesque, which would not be surprising in a 13th century town inhabited mainly by new immigrants from Normandy.

The White Friars pose a considerable mystery. They came to Bridport and were responsible for St Andrew's chapel; the support they received from the townspeople established them well and endowed their two organisations of St Mary and the Holy Trinity. They survived the conflicts which their presence provoked, and yet, in Carmelite records, they do not appear as an established organisation. An attempt to revive them in 1365 was frustrated. Perhaps it was the Black Death of 1348 which wiped them out, though an existence of over 80 years would surely not have escaped the records. Perhaps their chapel and its gilds were taken over, as the work of the ecclesiastical courts had been, by the secular authorities.

In 1361 the Bishop of Salisbury, Robert Wyvill, having come to Bridport to settle certain disputes which had arisen concerning St Andrew's chapel and the Rector of St Mary's, stated that he had found it to be the duty of the Rector to provide a chaplain for the chapel of St Andrew, and went on to describe the duties of that chaplain. This is curious. It is also curious that the Rector, the Bailiffs and the parishioners of Bridport had begged the Bishop to dedicate and consecrate the chapel of St Andrew which, they said, had been till then 'but a profane place'. In other words the former Bishop, at the time of the building of the chapel, had not complied with the request of the Papal Legate, and the chapel, in spite of all the observances which had taken place in it, had not had episcopal consecration. The word 'profane' may refer to secular control.

That settlement was not the end of the matter. Eighty years later there was a dispute between the Rector and the people because the former had not maintained a chaplain at St Andrew's nor allowed the chantry chaplain of St Katherine to celebrate Mass in St Mary's church. The new settlement may cast light, not only upon the earlier one, but upon the situation which followed the end of the Carmelite presence: for besides prescribing the Rector's duties, it recognised that those inhabitants who lived in the northern part of the town had the right to have Masses said for them, at their death and subsequently, in the chapel of St Andrew. So, although all parochial dues, including those collected at St Andrew's chapel, belonged now to the Rector, the tradition established at the time of the White Friars, whereby the new town used St Andrew's chapel as though it had been their parish church, was allowed to continue.

Further light is cast by an application made in 1365 by Sir John Chideock, Kt, for a licence to give three acres of land for a priory for Carmelite Friars, together with a mill, from which the profits would provide the means to celebrate Masses. A jury empanelled to consider the matter decided against it, on the grounds that it would be injurious to the patron and the rector of the parish church.

A letter of Pope Clement IV on 6 October 1268 commanded the Bishop, Dean and Chapter of Salisbury 'to desist from impeding the celebration of services by the Carmelites of Bridport'. This letter establishes the date of the building as 1261 and tends to confirm the origins and the difficulties.

In the Bridport archives there is a piece of paper which is no more than a list of names. Those names date the document to about 1600 and list men available for jury service. By a few of the names appears the phrase 'non jur'. Were these people ineligible for jury service, or had they refused to swear an oath—being non-jurors on principle? One case provides a clue. John Ellot, whose name appears on the list, had a daughter Priscilla born in 1608 and a son William born in 1613, so he was probably quite young when the list was drawn up. Among those who attended the General Meeting of the Society of Friends on 11 June 1688 were William Ellot senior and William Ellot junior, the son and grandson of the non-juror of c1600. This suggests that the refusal to swear an oath, though it came to be regarded as a Quaker peculiarity, probably had its origins, like Quakerism itself, in 16th century Puritanism. What the Sermon on the Mount forbad, the truthful man did not require. When William Ellot senior died in 1689, it was observed of him in the records of the Friends that he was 'one of the first to see the light'.

William Ellot senior would be about 44 years of age when George Fox came to Bridport and he was one of those who was predisposed, thanks to his father's influence, to welcome and adhere to the preacher. That visit is recorded in George Fox's journal.

'After this we came to Bridport, having meetings in the way. We went to an inn, and sent into the town for such as feared God; and there came a shopkeeper, a professor, and put off his hat to us, and seeing that we did not the same by him again, but said Thou and Thee to him, he told us "he was not of our religion"; and after some discourse with him he went away. Then he went and stirred up the priest and magistrates against us, and after a while sent to the inn to desire us to come to his house, for there were some that would speak with us, he said. Thomas Curtis was with me, and he went to the man's house; where, when he came, the man had laid a snare for him, and had got the priest and magistrate thither, and they boasted much that they had caught George Fox, taking him for me. When they perceived their mistake, they were in great rage; yet the Lord's power came over them, so that they let him go again. Meanwhile I had an opportunity of speaking to some sober people that came to the inn. When Thomas was come back, and we were passing out of the town, some of them came to us and said, "the officers were coming to fetch me"; but the Lord's power came over them all, so that they had not power to touch me. There were some convinced in the town, who were turned to the Lord, and have stood faithful to the Lord ever since, and a fine meeting there is there.'

Regular meetings of those who were 'faithful to the Lord' must have begun almost immediately, probably at first in the houses of members, though there was evidently a regular place of meeting as early as 1684. The earliest records reveal the names of those who were the backbone of the infant Society. Besides William Ellot and his son they included Thomas Bagg, Francis Williams, Humphry Sprague, Bartholomew Lugg, Hannah Nicholls, Elizabeth Osborne (whom William Ellot senior married in 1678) and, of course, Daniel Taylor.

We know a number of these names because of the difficulties experienced by the Society. From time to time their meetings were broken up and many of those present arrested and imprisoned. Undoubtedly they were helped by the fortitude shown by people like Daniel Taylor who, even while in prison, was busy with the Society's affairs. Thus in 1682 he wrote from Dorchester gaol promising £50 for the relief of poorer members. He was himself a successful merchant living in West Street (site now occupied by the International Supermarket) but also with property in South Street, opposite to the Parish Church. Here was a barn which in 1697 he gave to the Society for a permanent Meeting House. Here too he had a house with tenements behind, which he gave as almshouses for poor townspeople. He was the originator of a number of local charities, the best known being his educational foundation, which at one time provided a school from the profits of the Bull Hotel. When he died in 1714 his will provided for a great many beneficiaries, including 'my brother, Robert Swaisy....my sister, Mary Hardy....my sister, Hannah Smith....my cousin, Thomas Bagg....my sister, Abigail Sprague' and a great number of other 'cousins'. Whether we are to regard these as physical relationships or spiritual ones is not clear, but there are many bequests to members of the Society who are not so described. This is an interesting example of matrimonial patterns within a minority society. Taylor had two daughters married to John Nicholls and Elias Nicholls, and gave his clock to his grandson, John Nicholls, and £100 to his granddaughter, Mary Nicholls. It was typical of Taylor that his will included a bequest of £20 worth of wheat to the poor of Bridport.

The Society eventually established itself in the community and was able to play a full part in the life of the town. Not surprisingly, several members, besides Daniel Taylor and Thomas Bagg, were prominent in the business world. On the site now occupied by Boots the Chemist (13 East Street) there was Joseph Curtis, a merchant, possibly a grocer. He was followed on the same site in 1780 by Joseph Pike, then in 1797 by William Stephens, and eventually by the Reynolds family, a succession of Quaker families thus occupying one site over a considerable period. At 15 were the Westcombes, at 17 the Baggs and at 19 the Spragues. In addition, where Downes Street now divides the frontage, the business premises of Robert Bull and Daniel Taylor used to be. Thus for a time a small colony of Friends occupied a small section of the town's business centre. Though never a large community, a diocesan survey of 1766 assessing them as 14 families, they nevertheless played and still play an important part in the town's life.

A manuscript map of about 1770 shows the old shambles near the site of the former St Andrew's chapel. The tower of the chapel was still standing at this time and can be seen by rotating the page through 90 degrees clock-wise. It appears at the bottom right-hand corner of the centre square. (NR/B3/R2)

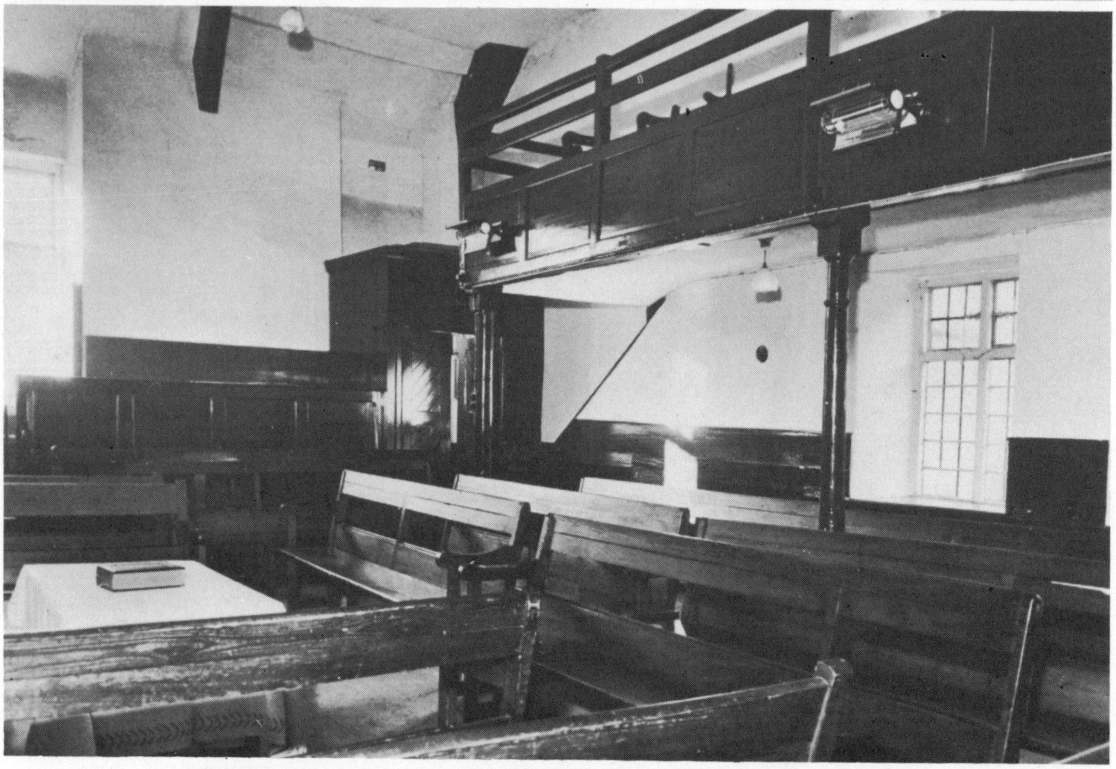

ABOVE: Properties in North Allington before their recent restoration, believed to be on the site of a house belonging to St Mary's Mass. (PEP/BM)
BELOW: Interior of the Friend's Meeting House prior to the alterations of 1958. (SF)

ABOVE: An old photograph of the Daniel Taylor Almshouses and some of the occupants. (SF) BELOW: The Society of Friends' new burial ground behind the Meeting House. (NR/SF)

Pictures found in Grahamstown, Cape Province, SA, by Harry Hudson of Burton Bradstock, and presented to the Museum. (Shephard/BM) ABOVE: West Street, c1870. INSET: East Street, c1870. BELOW: South Street, looking north, c1870.

Street Scene

The structure of the town was laid down a long time ago, and early forms are still visible. South Street was the spine of the Saxon town and its building line may tell a story. The widening of the street north of the church is probably due to the market. East and West Streets were the corresponding spine of the mediaeval town, and their shape suggests the location of the first market and of the bull ring. Into the former was inserted the chapel and priory of St Andrew; the latter was in front of the Bull inn. Even King Street has a long-standing topographical significance, as it was built on the line of a defensive ditch, part Saxon and part mediaeval.

The site immediately to the east of St Andrew's chapel was a valuable one, in the centre of the market which grew up around the chapel. Here, at the beginning of the 14th century, lived the family of Barri, or Barry. According to the taxation of 1315/6, Roger Barri had some interest in the local industry, his goods including flax and hemp, but 80 per cent of his taxable wealth was in wine. There were also Robert and John Barri, both involved in the rope and twine business. Roger appeared also in the taxations of 1319 and 1323. His widow, Lucy, made a will which was doubly proved in 1341, first in the diocesan court and then before the magistrates. The tavern which she had inherited from her husband had been leased to John the Hatter, another man with two occupations. Lucy had three daughters, all of whom made good marriages, Clarissa to Robert de Bemystre, Petronell to Peter the Goldsmith, and Alice to Robert of Assh. The property adjacent to St Andrew's chapel, including the tavern, was held by a later Robert de Bemynster who, being without an heir, left it in 1386 to his wife, Alice, for life (she died in 1400) and then to the bailiffs and community of Bridport for ever. Four hundred years later, as the Greyhound Inn, the property still belonged to the Borough, having been leased to a variety of tenants. In 1800 the freehold was purchased by the then leaseholder, William Pugsley Gummer. The inn probably became the Greyhound in Tudor times, when the silver greyhound was the badge of royal messengers.

In the 18th century fashion in building changed. Previously a good deal of cob was used for walls (locally called 'squab'). There is also evidence of timber framing. A certain amount of stone was employed, especially for front walls and also for the lowest courses of cob and half-timbered buildings. Thatch was commonly used for rooves.

In the 18th century brick was the fashionable building material, and was produced in a number of local brick-yards. Fires in thatched buildings probably hastened the process of change. But even houses which did not suffer this misfortune were brought up-to-date by face-lifting the front wall. There are cases of 17th century buildings with 18th century fronts. Thatch steadily disappeared, helped by a clause in the Market House Act, forbidding thatch on new buildings.

Although many buildings are more recent than the 18th century, the general style has persisted, and shows a remarkable continuity. We do not anticipate any eagerness to change its general character in the future.

ABOVE: South Street, looking south, c1870. (Shephard/BM) BELOW: The Greyhound as it appears in *Mate's Guide* of 1903. (BM) CENTRE: The Bull, then known as Knight's Bull, also in *Mate's Guide.* (BM) RIGHT: A Mate's picture of 1903 shows part of the lower front of the Golden Lion. (BM)

ABOVE: An East Street crowd listens to General Booth. (BM) BELOW: Old houses, Long's Court, West Street, now demolished. (BM)

ABOVE: West Street on a busy day. (BM) CENTRE: West Allington, looking west (BM) and BELOW: looking east. (Frith/BM)

ABOVE: King Street. (BM) BELOW: The leat, Folly Mill, showing the 'tin tabernacle' of Christ Church, Walditch. (Hider/BM)

ABOVE: East Mill. (BM) INSET: The doorway of Fullbrook House, N. Allington, now replaced by Cooper's Court. (A.W.J. Cobham/DM) BELOW: Downe Hall. (BM)

Ropes and Nets

For the Royal Navy Bridport used to mean rope. For many places in the world it still means nets—nets of all kinds: for fishing, for transport, for military camouflage, for tennis and football, and for any other conceivable use, including gardening.

The story goes back beyond available records, but it began with hemp and flax, two crops which grew well in this area, hemp in the rich alluvial valleys, flax on the hill slopes. It was natural for the district to thrive on the resultant products.

There was sailcloth, which was probably made at first of woven hemp, the word canvas derived from *cannabis.* Another important local woven product was the horse girth-web, frequently used as special gifts for visiting notables. There was twine, the twisted thread, *filum tortum,* mentioned in early taxations. There was also net, which has curiously little mention in early records, probably because it was mostly made for personal local use. In the same way twinespinning as an occupation is less mentioned than expected, presumably because nearly everyone did it as a secondary occupation and with family help.

So important was the industry that it affected local topography—not by making the main streets so wide, as is sometimes suggested; this was due, as in other places, to the existence of the markets; but rope and twine needed a 'walk', a long straight strip of ground. Hence there were good reasons for not developing the land behind the main street frontages. It was also useful to continue the style of building in which the house had a central passage from the street to the walk, the halves of the building often being separate dwellings. Along the length of the walk trees were usually planted, providing shade and perhaps fruit, and also supporting the 'skirders', upright fingers which kept the strands separate. At the far end was the 'turn-house' where the 'jack' was housed to twist the thread.

The earliest local references appear in the 13th century, notably the command of King John in 1213 that ropes should be made 'night and day...for ships both large and small...and twisted yarns for cordage for ballistae'. Thus began a long story of provision for the navy, lasting for several centuries. As an example, in the 14th century, although a small amount of rope for the navy was produced at Yarmouth, the main supplier of black, white and bastard thread and rope was Bridport. This virtual monopoly was broken in the 15th century, but in the time of Henry VIII it was still claimed that the supply had continued 'time out of mind'.

Not surprisingly Bridport developed its own standards of quality, its own measures of length and weight, its own methods of production and its own language to describe materials, measures and methods.

Although this was (and to some degree still is) a cottage industry, quite early the trade in the finished goods was organised by middlemen. One of these was William Bume, and certain local men dealt with naval supplies. Rope-making was more demanding than twine-making, and so it was a trade calling for apprenticeships, along with tailoring, felt-making, saddlery, shoe-making, milling, tallow-chandlery, joinery and weaving, but twine-spinning and net-making do not appear in the list. Thus in 1572 Henry Stone, a farmer's son, was apprenticed to Richard Hounsell, a rope-maker, and eventually became a rope-maker on his own account. This could have been a long apprenticeship, for in 1608 John Tucker, aged 4 years, was apprenticed to John Elliott, rope-maker, until the age of 21.

Several members of the Hounsell family appear as rope-makers in the 16th century, and early in the 17th century the Gundry family came on the scene. In 1624 John Gundry, a feltmaker, married Lydia More and had a daughter, Lydia, and two sons, John and Samuel. It was through Samuel and then through his grandson, Joseph, that the twine and net business developed, the first home and place of business being 48 West Street. The interests of the family were quite wide, the most usual description of this line being 'maltster'. Brewing continued to be an interest even in the 18th century, when the main business was well developed. Meanwhile the Hounsells were establishing themselves to the east of Stake Lane (Barrack Street) before branching out into other parts of the town and district. William Hounsell's foreman, Eli Stembridge, lived in Stake Lane (now 22 Barrack Street) and saw the development first of Wykes Court and then of North Mills, where he went to live at No 1. Ensuring an adequate supply of local labour was a preoccupation of John Hounsell, who built houses for twine-spinners in Stake Lane and whose son, William, in difficult times, supplemented charity payments to unemployed spinners from his own pocket. Although most of the work was still in the cottages, the larger employers set up twine-walks, drying grounds and warehouses. Even before the end of the 18th century machine-spinning by water-power had been introduced by Rendall & Coombs at Burton Bradstock, and it was not long afterwards that netting looms appeared. Although there were several manufacturing firms, some specialising in particular products, amalgamations took place from about 1910. Shortly after the end of the second world war there were two main combines, Joseph Gundry & Co, and Bridport Industries Ltd. Since 1963 these have been combined as Bridport-Gundry Ltd.

The machinery is much improved and is now concentrated in factories at the Court and North Mills. The materials used have changed with the introduction of man-made fibres. But, although the business is centralised, there is still a good deal of outwork to deal with those parts of the manufacturing process in which fingers are more nimble and adaptable than machines.

Bridport has never aspired to become another Birmingham, Detroit or Cowley, but it has made a small contribution in their fields.

Surprisingly there have been several foundries in the town. The earliest was that of John Dollin in East Street, but there were also the Wadhams in Rax Lane, Helyear of West Street, Harris of Foundry Lane, Sprake of Allington, Samsons, the Paragon and, still operating, the Grove Iron Works in West Road. Iron was imported by sea from Stockton, to be turned into useful and ornamental ironwork, some of which can still be seen in railings and rain-water goods.

The coming of the motor-car inspired, not an industry but a hobby, a side-line to the more important business of making marine engines. Edwin Chard, of St Andrews Road, decided in the early 20th century to apply his engineering knowledge and skill to the popular novelty. His first 'Brit' was an 8 horse-power model. He supplied an engine to John Hunt in 1903 to power Beaminster's first car, and the first Brit to be registered, when registration was introduced in 1904, was FX 100. Subsequently a 12 hp tourer was made, four examples identifiable by registration. Then Chard lost interest and went back to his engines for boats, which are still made by Brit Engineering of St Andrews Road.

Ropes, twines and nets may be the staple of the town and district, but other things have also occupied people's time and effort. There were public services and there were the shops.

There was also the coming of the railway.

The Bridport branch was born in 1857 and died in 1975. The venture was the product of local initiative, served a useful purpose for over a century, but fell victim to the same impulse which produced it—the force called progress. Yet there must be many who recall with regret a delightful rural ride, offering vistas not to be seen by the motorist, and of course linking our little town with the countrywide network of British Rail.

There are further facets of Bridport life besides industry. There is a considerable cultural tradition, particularly with music. The Arts Society has its own premises, the former Wesleyan chapel, while the Bridport and West Dorset Music Society has a large and growing membership. Drama, film, painting, all have their place in our life, and a past.

There are still lighter sides to our life, and some of that is to be found in old pictures. If now we travel far afield for our outings and picnics, there was a time when paradise was called Happy Island or Eype Down.

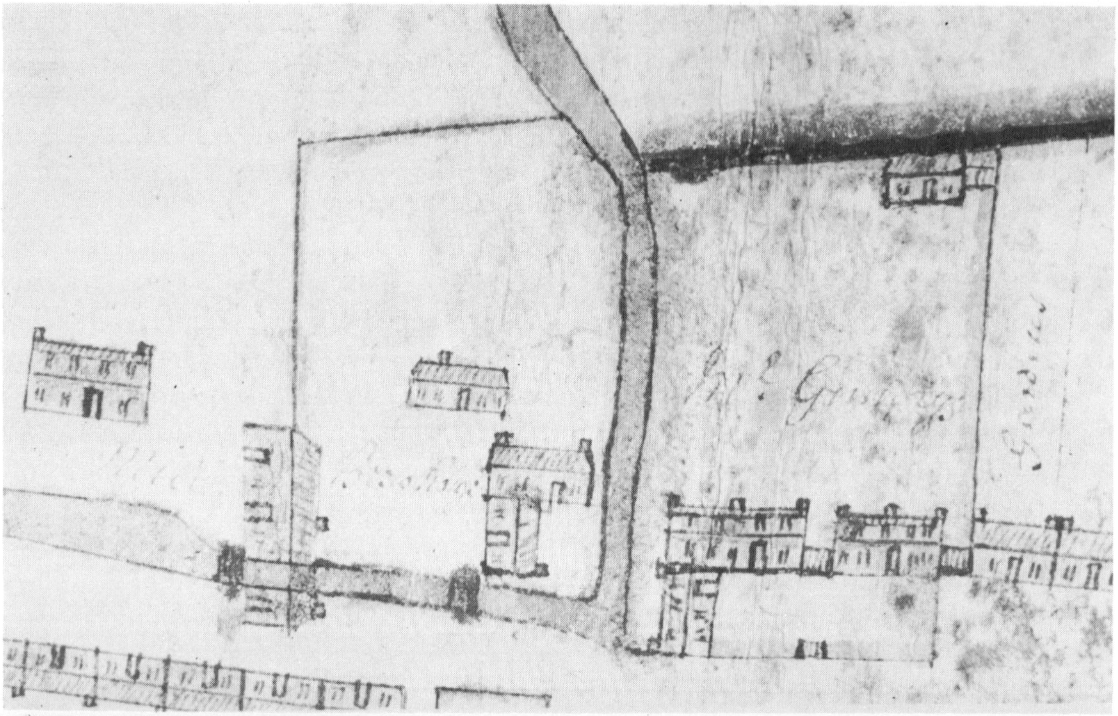

ABOVE LEFT: Another part of the 1770 MS map. showing West Mill, the Brewhouse and Mr Gundry's (The Court). (NR/B3/R2) BELOW: Flax retting — steeping in water to soften the outer case of the fibre. (BM) OPPOSITE ABOVE LEFT: Stooking the retted flax. (BM) RIGHT: Heckling. (BM) OPPOSITE CENTRE LEFT: Sorting dressed flax. (BM) RIGHT: A Bridport braider on a trade-calendar. (BG) OPPOSITE BELOW: Francis Newberry's picture of twine-making, part of a mural in the town hall. (BTC)

ABOVE LEFT: Mrs Jessie Butcher braiding. (JH) RIGHT: Olive Legg of Loders, outworker. (BM) BELOW: Outdoor braiders, Loders. (BM)

ABOVE: Mrs Greening makes a pig-net, Mrs Poole a rick-net. (BM)
BELOW: The early 'jumper' looms — man-powered. (BM)

ABOVE: Power looms — woman-controlled. (BM) BELOW: Light and air in a modern factory. (BG)

ABOVE: Hand machine braiders, Joseph Gundry & Co, 1910. (BM) CENTRE: Another group of Gundry workmen. (BM) BELOW: Braiders outside Gundry's. (BM)

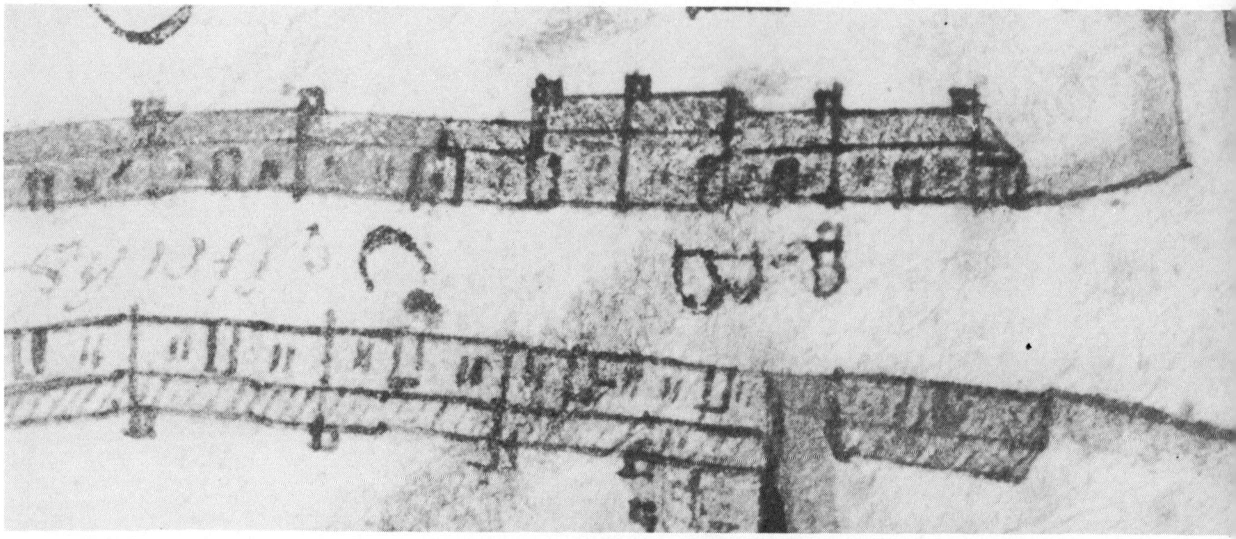

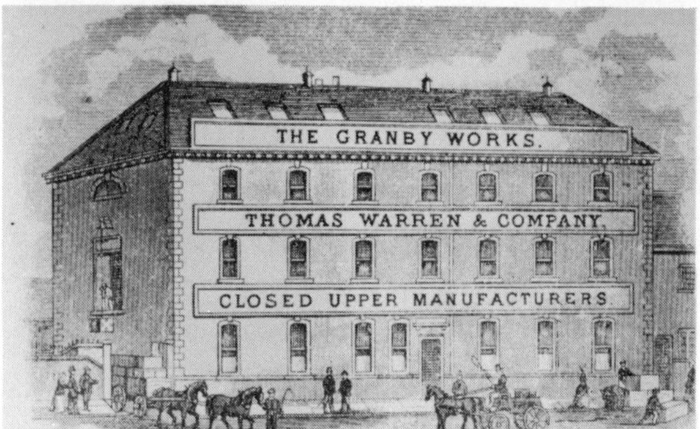
THE GRANBY WORKS.
THOMAS WARREN & COMPANY.
CLOSED UPPER MANUFACTURERS.

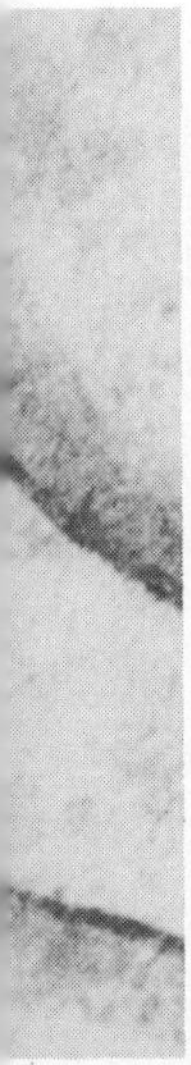

ABOVE LEFT: Another section of the 1770 MS map, showing houses in Stake Lane (Barrack Street) built by John Hounsell for twine spinners, and the cause of a dispute between the parishes of Bridport and Bradpole. (NR/B3/R2) RIGHT: Pymore Mills. (BM) CENTRE: An old picture of North Mills, the former Allington corn-mill converted by William Hounsell. (BM) LEFT: The Court, formerly the headquarters of Joseph Gundry & Co, now of Bridport Gundry Ltd. (BM) (BM) BELOW LEFT: Thomas Warren's factory, formerly the Marquis of Granby. (BM) RIGHT: The railway 'bus about to depart. (BM)

ABOVE: The post 'bus. CENTRE: The Royal Mail. BELOW: The Post Office staff, c1912. (BM)

ABOVE: The sorting office, c1912. BELOW: Bridport Gas Co, South Street. INSET: Municipal Electric Power Station, built by George Abbot & Son, and opened in 1929. (BM)

ABOVE: Sheep-shearing, Askerswell, c1900. (BM)
CENTRE: Hurdle-making, Askerswell, c1900. (BM)
LEFT: Fooks, 19 South Street. (BM)

ABOVE: Bothenhampton quarry. (BM) BELOW: Reynolds', East Street (now Boots the Chemist). (BM)

Two Reynolds' interiors. (BM)

ABOVE: Mr Edward Simmonds, West Street, in his doorway. Mrs Irene Simmonds (nee Roberts) in upper window. (BM) BELOW: George Bonfield, East Street, an early motoring enthusiast on far left. (BM) ABOVE RIGHT: Stembridge's, South Street (now Palace Cinema); (BM) BELOW: Roberts & Sons, West Allington. (BM) CENTRE: Roberts & Sons, 30 West Street, after moving from West Allington. Miss Linda Roberts at door. (BM) BELOW: Wilson Hansford and Ford van, registered FX4297, 1919. (BM)

ABOVE LEFT: John Hoare, grocer, West Allington. (BM) RIGHT: W. Medway, leather cutter and legging manufacturer, East Street. (BM) CENTRE LEFT: The Ship and the saddlery, South Street, 1910. (BM) RIGHT: Hine Bros, 40 East Street. (BM) LEFT: Lion head, found on several rainwater gutters and probably a local foundry product. (NR/BM) RIGHT: Bridport's motor-car the *Brit*, pictured on Edwin Chard's bill-head. (BM)

TOWN-HALL, BRIDPORT.

THE BRIDPORT

Harmonic Society

WILL GIVE THEIR THIRD

VOCAL AND INSTRUMENTAL

CONCERT

THIS SEASON, ON

Thursday Evening, March 27th, 1845,

On which occasion the Hall will, for the first time, be brilliantly illuminated with Gas from the new and splendid Chandeliers, lately suspended.

LEADER, MR. WILLIAM MOORE.

PROGRAMME.

PART FIRST.

OVERTURE, "William Tell," .... *Rossini.*
SET OF QUADRILLES, "Jack Sheppard," .... *Musard.*
GLEE, THREE VOICES, "The Red Cross Knight,"...... .... *Calcott.*
SET OF WALTZES, "Deutsche Lust," .... *Strauss.*
GLEE, FOUR VOICES, "Hail Smiling Morn," .... *Spofforth*
OVERTURE, "Lodoiska," .... *Kreutzer.*

PART SECOND.

OVERTURE, "Guy Mannering," .... *Bishop.*
SET OF QUADRILLES, "The Transatlantic," .... *Jullien.*
GLEE, THREE VOICES, "The Gypsies' Glee," .... *Reeve.*
SOLO, FLUTE, (Piano Forte Accompaniment,) .... *Nicholson.*
SET OF QUADRILLES, "The Royal Hunt," .... *Jullien.*
GLEE, FOUR VOICES, "The Merriest Time of all the Year," .... *Aldridge.*
GRAND PIECE BY BRASS BAND, "Love Not," arranged by .... *Purton.*

Doors to be opened at seven. Performance to commence at Half-past seven.

TICKETS, Front Seats, 2s., or Family Tickets to admit Four, 6s. Back Seats, 1s.

To be had at M. TUCKER & SON'S, Mr. PRINCE'S, or Mr. EBDON'S.

M. TUCKER & SON, PRINTERS, SOUTH STREET, BRIDPORT.

A concert notice of 1845 — with new illumination, by gas! (BM)

ABOVE: Bridport Choral and Orchestral Society, 1905-6 season: Haydn, 'The Creation'; Alex Stone, conductor. (E.C. Hare/BM) CENTRE: Independent Order of Good Templars Orchestra, 1906: Stephen Champ (Mayor), conductor. (BM) BELOW: Mrs Colfox firing the first shot, Bridport Rifle Club, September, 1906. (BM)

ABOVE: Concert at the Unitarian Sunday School. BELOW: Bridport Carnival, August 1923. (W.H. Hann)

ABOVE: Bridport Football Club, 1913. (W.H. Hann) CENTRE: 1 September, 1927: W. S. Edwards in charge, but of what? (BM) BELOW: The Unitarian choir on a day out.

ABOVE: A Unitarian picnic on Eype Down. BELOW: Happy Island, a much-loved picnic spot. (BM)

ABOVE: All the fun of the fair, West Bay Road fairground, c1911. (BM)
BELOW: E. Roberts and Sons outing c1920; the charabanc loaded outside Balsons' butcher's shop, West Allington. (BM) Left to right, top: Mr Garfield, George Roberts, C. Bond, Dan Roberts, Mrs E. Roberts, W. Garland, Miss Dimmick, Mrs W. Garland, Miss K. Bowers, Nancy Garland, T. Dimmick, Mrs T. Dimmick, Sylvia Roberts, Miss G. Taylor, Miss D. Barrett, centre: Frank Roberts, Joyce Roberts, Ivor Bond, Miss L. Roberts, Mrs C. Bond, W. Hansford, bottom: Ron Taylor, Tom Patten, George Ward, Arthur Gerrard, Master Hansford, Mrs W. Hansford.

ABOVE: Bonfield's chara takes the Unitarians for their outing. (BM) CENTRE: St Mary's bell-ringers ready for their outing. (BM) LEFT: West Bay Station in the 1880's. (BM)

ABOVE: West Bay Station, 1910. (BM) CENTRE: Bridport Station on a busy day in 1914. (BM) BELOW: And it came to this! (MJT)

Health and Hazard

Europe cannot surely have suffered a more dreadful calamity than the Black Death. In the scale of mortality it exceeded any of the wars of this continent. Measured by its consequences it achieved more than any of the revolutions, even the French or the Russian. It completed the breakdown of the feudal system and created the need for new economic and political methods. It deeply undermined the position of the Church, paving the way for the Reformation by raising new theological issues. Yet there is such a deficiency of evidence, that historians have made widely varying estimates of its impact. The number who died, for instance, has been given as low as 10 per cent or as high as 50 per cent of the total population.

The evidence which Bridport might provide is by no means slight. Bridport through its magistrates proved its own wills. Great care was taken of the records including a reasonable number of 14th century wills. These are the years and number of wills: 1313, 1339, 1346, 1347, 1348 (16), 1349 (2), 1358, 1361 (5), 1362 (2), 1367, 1369, 1371 (2), 1374 (3), 1375, 1381, 1384 (2), 1385 (2), 1386, 1390, 1391, 1395, 1396 (2), 1398, 1400. A serious calamity occurred in 1348, and there were minor disasters in 1361 and 1374. In fact the Black Death belonged to the years 1348 and 1349, and the first return of the Plague, as it was subsequently called, was in 1361, with several other outbreaks later.

The proportion of 18 Black Death wills out of a total of 52 wills extant from the 14th century is remarkable. But this is not the only evidence. The White Friars may have been wiped out; but there were other clergy. At the parish church of St Mary there were four rectors at the time of the Black Death. Peter de Colyngton died, and his successor was instituted in November 1348. He had a successor named Henry, who also died and was followed in February 1349 by William de Hampine. Few churches can ever have had such a rapid turnover. Sadly, William de Hampine died in 1361. He had a successor who resigned almost immediately and was followed by John Cok.

In 1348 the bailiffs of Bridport were Edward Stone and John Grey. Both died and were replaced by William Hychecoke and Richard Laurenz. In 1361 these two replacements of the Black Death year died of the Plague. This William Hychecoke had two colleagues, Edward Coterich and John Tracy, who represented the Bridport ropemakers in the business of supplying rope for the King's navy. One of these colleagues, Edward Coterich, died in the Plague of 1361; the other died in 1384, which may also have been a Plague year in the town.

Bearing in mind that these were the leading men of the town, we are forced to the conclusion that, if they were no more than representative of the general mortality (though the risks may have been higher among the poor), then the Black Death was a major catastrophe, and the death rate in the Black Death years of 1348-9 was at least 50 per cent, and still heavy in the years of the Plague.

The Black Death must have given added significance to the work of the parish gilds. Gilds existed at least as early as the 12th century, including those connected with St Andrew's chapel soon after its foundation. It is to the 15th century that we turn for any considerable account of what the gilds did and their membership. The first record is dated 1399.

One function of a gild was to provide lighting for the church or for one of its individual altars. No doubt it was for this reason that membership dues and fines were paid, in part at least, in wax. It also explains why each gild was named according to the particular purpose of the lights. The gilds attached to the parish church were of the Light hanging before the Cross, of the Torches, of the Two Torches, of the Mortuary Light, of St Nicholas and of St Katherine, in the case of St Andrew's chapel, those of St Mary and St James and of Holy Cross. There was also a gild of St Mary, which may have been a continuation of the St Andrew's gild of the late 13th century, but to which of the two churches it was attached is not clear.

Another function of the gilds was to provide a kind of insurance for the members. In the case of death they could be sure of decent burial and of masses said for their departed souls. A curiously modern provision, however, was contained in the rule: 'It was also ordained that if any brother or sister of the said fraternity shall come to such poverty that he has not the means of maintaining himself, that he shall receive weekly from the wardens 3d or 4d or more that he may be maintained'. (Holy Cross Rules.)

In the case of a few of the gilds there are rules, membership lists and accounts. For most of them there are names and accounts, and for some there are records of gild property. There is sufficient to compile a list of several hundred inhabitants. Some were members of two or even three gilds, possibly at the same time. The names of many of the chaplains who were attached to each gild are on record too.

In the accounts of one gild the weight of wax prescribed for a candle, or 'torch', was 26 lbs, which means that it was a thick candle four or five feet high. For domestic lighting they probably had to be content with tallow.

One rule may have foreshadowed the sad fate of some gilds. 'Also each brother and sister shall come after sunset and shall say a Paternoster and an Ave Maria for the deceased brother or sister and there, at the expense of the deceased, they shall drink once, and there shall they remain until their names are marked.' Drinking together was a custom which tended to grow, and other occasions were found for enjoying it, as for example in the parish 'ales' in honour of particular saints. Thus, on the Wednesday of Easter week 23 April 1477, ale was sold in honour of St George the Martyr. The account rendered on 4 May by the stewards, Richard Orchard and John Hulle, showed a clear profit of 19 shillings. 'They had also received in moneys beforehand 6s

8d.' This represents an enormous quantity of ale, for it is likely that the supplier(s) also had a share of the profit. Richard Orchard may have been an innkeeper—perhaps of the George. Some gilds degenerated into drinking clubs, and in this Bridport was not unusual.

William Olyver, a member of the gilds of St Mary and St Katherine, many times Bailiff of the borough, in 1454 collected from many of the gilds the money to buy two anthem books 'for our Lady Church of Bridport'. The sum collected was £11 11s 4d, which Olyver took to London to purchase the books, his agent there, or possibly the bookseller, being John Wacle of Bread Street in the Barbican.

Incidentally William Olyver's account mentions two other gilds,of St Thomas and of 'the Light called Branch'.

The Black Death may have been the worst scourge experienced by the inhabitants of Bridport, but they had many other serious epidemics. The parish registers record outbreaks of plague. A note in August 1626 reads: 'from this place unto Anne d. of Maut Shootte those following died of the plague'. Then follow 82 names, finishing with Anne, daughter of Maud Shootte and a further note: 'this is a lie that was the last that died of the plaug'. People were dying almost every day from 18 August to the end of October, whole families succumbing. The first victim was Martha, daughter of George Lumbard. The latter and five of his sons died at the end of August. Bennett Pratt lost his wife and two daughters. Robert Miller, his wife and two daughters died, as did Robert Keat, his wife and four children. Outbreaks of small-pox and cholera were also recorded.

This kind of experience was probably quite common in other towns, but here there are specific causes of ill-health. Until fairly recently, urban societies worked on a do-it-yourself basis for many purposes, including rubbish and waste disposal. It was expected of the householder that he would arrange for the disposal of all his wastes, and the courts endeavoured, with less than complete success, to compel him to do so. Case after case appears in the records of people summoned for allowing 'noisome dung mixons' to remain near their front doors. One interesting case occurred on 11 April 1637: 'we present George Sydnam for casting out his filthy Excrements in the streat by St Andrews for the annoyance his neybors and is daungerous for infection'. That last phrase suggests that there was already some awareness of the issue of public health.

Another danger probably lay in dependence upon local wells for the supply of drinking water. The hazard of this was illustrated by a recent excavation near Chancery Lane. Here a domestic cess-pit had been built partly over the shaft of a mediaeval well. The introduction of cess-pits may have helped the problem of disposal, but exposed the water supply to other dangers.

This unsatisfactory state of affairs continued for a long time, until, in the early 19th century, there was a national drive to improve urban health. This has a curious connection with Bridport in that one of the pioneers of public health was Dr T. Southwood Smith (1788-1861) who was born in Somerset, became a Unitarian minister, and later went to Edinburgh to train as a doctor. From Yeovil he came to

Bridport to preach a memorial sermon for Rev Thomas Howe, first minister of the New Chapel in East Street. He became an authority on fevers and the associate of Edwin Chadwick in the campaign for the Public Health Act of 1848. Implementation of the Act by town councils was (except in the worst cases) optional. Consequently health became a local political issue, some working for radical reform, others sharing the opinion of the *Times:* 'We prefer to take our chance of Cholera and the rest than be bullied into health'. Appropriately the reform movement in Bridport was spear-headed by one of Howe's successors, Rev J. Lettis Short. In a lecture given at the town hall on 20 March 1849 he gave a thorough account of mortality statistics in the counties and towns of the land, and suggested that Bridport's record was far from satisfactory. Housing density was too high, drainage was quite inadequate, there was a shortage of privies, the parish church burial ground was too small, and the water supply was in many places impure and poisonous. There was considerable support, his lecture being printed as a pamphlet. A popular version of his argument appeared, entitled 'The Cholera found where it isn't seen', and with a preface by 'Drs Cleanhouse and Pureair, and Professors Washwell and Hateslop, Directors of the Board of Health'.

There was considerable opposition to reform and progress was delayed. Eventually the Medical Department of the Privy Council decided to intervene, and in 1864 they sent a Dr Buchanan to report on the sanitary conditions. His account makes extremely unpleasant reading, but it shows the thoroughness of his investigation. He concluded that the piping in of fresh water from outside the town was a pressing need, but that even more urgent was to have the town 'purified from the mass of putrid matter that lies in its privy vaults and poisons the air by its decomposition'. The local Board of Health was eager to act (or at least a majority was) and a survey was commissioned to look into the question of water supply. Popular support was encouraged by satire, both in song and, when Dr Buchanan came again in 1870 in response to a petition signed by 112 local people, in the following poem in the local paper.

Oh, ye men of Bridport, is this your Christian state?
Is the health of all these families not worth a shilling rate?
Shall Dorchester and Weymouth with good water be supplied,
And wealthy Bridport have this common right denied?
While other towns move forward, in the lurch shall we be found,
And whilst we're wise in pennies, be foolish by the pound?
Look forward a few years, then a penny rate you'll see,
And with water everyone as pleased as pleased can be.
You're ready with your help when sickness strikes a neighbour;
Be wise! improve his health, and for himself he'll labour.
From port wine and doctor's bills the shilling let us take,
And save in pain and fever and every sort of ache,
And we'll gain our shilling back, in energy and nerve,
And in thankfulness of heart that others we can serve.

To him that humbly asks, a cup of water give,
And Christ Himself has told that such a deed shall live.

Dr Buchanan's second report was critical of the little progress made, and blamed the opposition for aiming at 'inaction and delay'. The Privy Council Medical Department therefore asked the Secretary of State to intervene, using powers vested in him by the Sanitary Act.

Very soon things changed. A water company was set up in 1872 and soon piped fresh water from Litton Cheney. The improvement of drains was speeded up. The saddest footnote, however, is that the only reform completed before Lettis Short left Bridport in 1864 was the new cemetery in East Road, and his own son was one of the first burials. He himself was buried here in 1876.

One of the obvious dangers in a town where most of the houses were thatched was the risk of fire. Fires varied in their destructive effect, but it was by no means unusual for several houses to be involved. For example, a gap in the rating returns suggests that a fire in West Street, on the site now occupied by West End Dairy, Milne & Lyall, and Portman Building Society, occurred in 1773. The first of these houses was rebuilt within a year, but it was not until 1776 that the others again paid rates. About a year or so after this fire there was one on the other side of West Street, destroying Joseph Gundry's malt-house on the site now occupied by Rees's shoe shop. This was rebuilt in 1775. There were a number of fires in the late 18th century, as insurance records show, for it was in that century that the Sun Fire Office established a branch here, and recently some records relating to local fires were found in the basement of the Genealogical Society's headquarters.

One such fire broke out in South Street at about one o'clock in the morning of Wednesday, 19 April, 1780, and so frightened the merchants of East and West Streets, in case it should spread, that they persuaded their insurance agent to allow them to recruit a large number of men to deal with it, although the premises immediately involved seem not to have been insured. Over 80 people fought the blaze, 'which raged with great Fury for a considerable Time', and others kept watch on the two succeeding nights in case smouldering thatch should cause further trouble. Each man received two shillings for his night's work, and was refreshed by liquor supplied by the Five Bells (the present Museum), the Royal Oak, (then on the south side of West Street), the Higher and the Lower Cross Keys, the George and the Swan (now the Book Shop). The total cost to the insurance company was twopence under fifteen pounds, including cleaning the engine and lost buckets and pails. The names of all these men, otherwise unrecorded except in parish registers, are listed. Apart from a few they were not ratepayers, probably because of poverty, and some are listed elsewhere as recipients of charity. Yet Thomas Hutchins, David Gale, William Patten, John Stone, John Champ, Henry Welch, George Hussey, John Kenway, John Hallett and many more with good local names, had their night's work put on record in the annals of the Fire Office.

That Office was probably glad to pay only £15. Two years later a fire at the Guildhall, most of which was leased by T. C. Colfox, cost them almost £1,000. The house next door, occupied by Mrs Ann Denziloe, a milliner, was also involved and cost them over £300. Mr Colfox repaired his building, replacing it later by building Stagg House, demolished not many years ago to give us Lipton's building. Mrs Denziloe's replacement still stands (Christina's Fashions) and the unaltered parts suggest that the builder was David Fudge, for the brickwork reflects his style. Perhaps it was this that earned him the contract to build the Town Hall, the Guildhall's replacement on a new site, three years later.

When a Parliamentary Bill was presented to enable the building of the Town Hall, it included a new regulation forbidding thatch on any new building, though to replace it on older buildings was still permitted. As time passed it was fire which was mainly responsible for the disappearance of thatch. Much of it went during the 19th century, a notable instance being on the building which was replaced by 'Kendall's Corner', by the Town Hall.

There is one fire which is still remembered, involving Miss Gundry's thatched Infants' School, burnt down in 1906. It was a building with a long history, its earliest known use being educational. In 1650 the malt-house and brewhouse belonging to Thomas Bartlett and his son were acquired by the trustees of the will of Jane Napper and handed over to the bailiffs and burgesses, the income to be used for the poor of the Borough, especially for educating the young and apprenticing them. The buildings remained Borough property until 1865, when Joseph Gundry bought them for £600. The site is now a car-park of Bridport-Gundry Ltd.

Flood years come every now and again, either by the breaking in of the sea, the last serious case being half a dozen years ago, or by the overburdening of the rivers Brit and Asker, as happened in 1979.

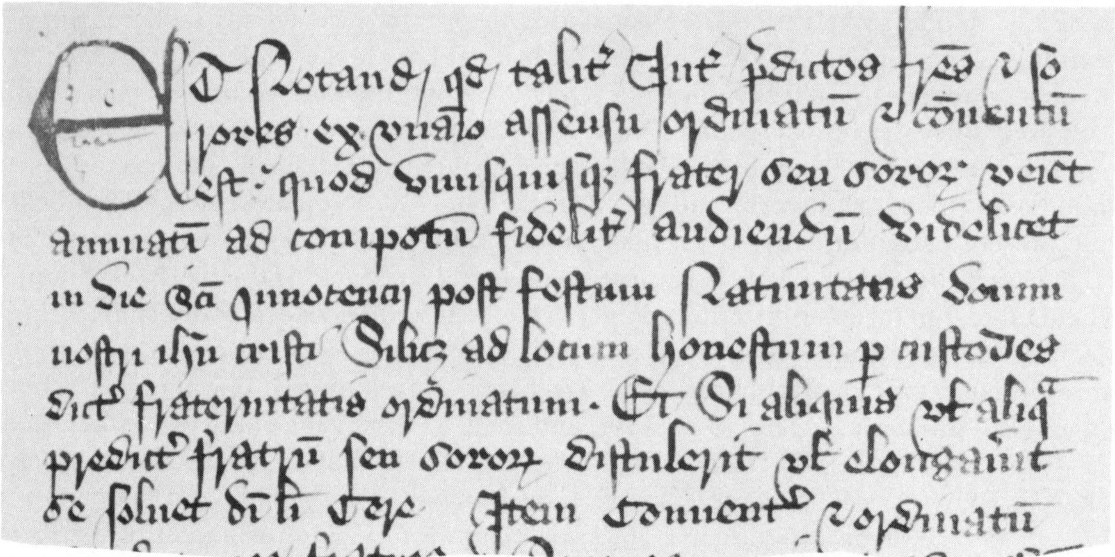

Rules of the gild of St Nicholas of St Mary's church. (NR(B3/CD14)

A SONG

FOR THE

MEN OF BRIDPORT.

I likes the smell of dirt,
It seems to do me good;
It raises up my spirits
And relishes my food.

A dung-hill at my door
And a cess-pool close at hand
Is the healthiest things in nature,
The sweetest in the land.

'Tis nice to see my children
Sitting down in filth and mire,
And their clothes in dirty patches
Is all I could desire.

A shilling and three-halfpence
I likes to pay for pills;
'Tis nicer and 'tis better
Than giving up the "smills."

For water in my house
Flowing nicely from a tap,
Pure, clean, and bright, and sparkling,
I should'nt care a rap.

I likes a great deal better
To draw it from a well,
Looking yellow, tasting strongly,
With a nice good drainy smell.

It makes the clothes look muddy,
And the colour is'nt good,
But it is'nt bad in tea
Or mixed up in my food.

Up then, ye men of Bridport!
Get all the smells ye may:
For dirty courts and sickness,
Hip, hip, hip, hip, Hurray!

PRINCE, PRINTER AND STATIONER, BRIDPORT.

A broadsheet of 1864. (NR/B3/MN21)

ABOVE: The new cemetery in East Road. (MT/BM) BELOW: Bridport Fire Brigade, 1897. (BM)

ABOVE: The Fire Brigade during celebrations of the coronation of Edward VII (1901). The man on the tricycle is Job Legg, formerly proprietor of Bridport Brewery. BELOW: A famous fire of 1906, the burning of Miss Gundry's Infant School, formerly the charity brewhouse. (BM)

ABOVE: The School fire in 1906, showing the Merryweather engine hard at work. (BM) BELOW: A fire at West Bay, 1970. Here the thatch is being removed. (PEP/BM)

West Bay fire, c1920, affecting Pier Terrace. (BM) INSET: The Brigade acquires a new engine in 1926. The chief officer, E. S. Reynolds, stands on the running board. (BM)

Clearing up after a fire at Hooke. (PEP/BM) INSET: The old Merryweather engine returns from the scrap-heap in 1960, thanks to F. G. Parker, who restored it and presented it to the town. It was displayed at West Bay in a specially made show-case. (BM)

ABOVE: West Street in the 1929 flood. (BM) BELOW: Aftermath — mud! (BM)

ABOVE LEFT: The triumphal archway at the top of South Street. (BM) RIGHT: Captain Templer and his neice, Hebe. (DMM) BELOW: The volunteers' camp on the cliffs. (BM)

Riflemen, Arm!

From time to time Bridport has been disturbed by fears of invasion. One occasion was early in the 13th century, when Philip of France was threatening. Another was in 1859 when war in Italy, with Britain opposed to French policies there, led to fears that Napoleon III might invade. This threat was taken seriously, and by none more than the mayor, Henry Augustus Templer, of The Grove, Rax Lane. He wrote a letter to the *Dorset County Chronicle* and then published it as a poster, with a list of his principal supporters in the town.

'SIR, — "Riflemen, Arm!" is a call which cannot fail to arouse all PATRIOTS. It is a cry not for war but for peace. It is a warning for preparation, and a significant notice that those who neglect the preparation may be summoned by the actual war-cry when it is too late. Such a call had been uttered by our Queen, through the voice of her Minister, and ere this it has reached the ear of every hamlet in our Island. Let it be nobly answered. It is an appeal for what? — not the acquisition of territory — not the intermingling with foreign quarrels — not the elevation of the weak or the subjection of the strong — but an appeal to shield with power our aged and infirm, our sisters, our wives and defenceless children, our household Gods and our Homes ...'

There followed an appeal that the volunteers, expected to be mainly working-class, should be armed by a Volunteers' Fund, raised by subscriptions by 'the aristocracy and landed gentry, the clergy, the merchant and manufacturer, whose position, prosperity, and property are the objects of protection'.

Some of the support was in the form of patriotic verse. Thus Rev S. C. Malan, of Broadwindsor, wrote the following for the *Bridport News*.

'THE BRIDPORT VOLUNTEERS

The gallant men of Bridport
Have taken up their arms,
To defend their wives and sisters,
Their shops, and eke their farms.
The first of all the Dorset men
To calm their country's fears!
O! some of England's bravest
Are the Bridport Volunteers!

Just fancy what a comfort 'tis
At Osborne, for the Queen,
To know her gallant Bridport men
Have donned the Rifle green!
And fancy how the Emperor
Must tremble when he hears
Of the valiant Captain Templer
And his band of Volunteers!

I wonder where the men will be
of other coward towns,
When the bearded little Zouaves
Come marching o'er the downs?
When the strains of martial music
Come pealing in our ears,
How every man would wish he'd joined
The Bridport Volunteers!

So all you men of Dorset,
Enrole while yet you may,
And learn the drill and how to shoot,
Before the evil day;
And ladies, in conclusion,
We'll wave three hearty cheers,
For the lion-hearted Templer,
And his gallant Volunteers.'

The Bridport Volunteers encamped on the cliffs and kept watch, pioneers in a movement which eventually led to the formation of the Territorial Army. In fact nothing happened, but this successful defence of our shores was thought worthy of celebration.

ABOVE: Archways in West Bridge (BM) and BELOW: in East Street. (BM)

So Busy a Man

A town's past is reflected in its people and their achievements. *The Man of Law's Book* — a tattered and worm-drilled volume — belonged to Richard Laurenz, or Lawrence, a busy and important townsman of the 14th century.

The book contains transcripts of many early Parliamentary statutes, covering a wide variety of legal matters, from religion to marketing. There are also sample drafts of legal forms and details of how deeds should be drawn up, with a model inventory of the contents of a rich man's house. There are many local matters, such as the foundation charters of local chantries, maritime rights of the borough, a list of bailiffs from 1312 to 1361, and some proceedings in the local courts.

One personal item is the record of the birth of Laura, second daughter of Richard and Petronilla Laurenz, on the eve of St Petronilla the Virgin in 1338.

Richard Laurenz, who was responsible for some of the legal business following the Black Death in 1348-9, seems to have been a victim of the first recurrence of the Plague in 1361-2.

From books to learning: it would not be surprising if some young men of the town went up to study at the University of Oxford, a fairly new institution. There were no colleges, both the Masters and the students living in lodgings and meeting for lectures and seminars in any convenient place, usually a tavern. One who certainly went up was known as Giles de Bridport, a man who later rose rapidly in the Church and eventually became Bishop of Salisbury. As well as completing the building of the cathedral he created an institution, Vaux College, or the Schools of the Valley of Sarum, in order to bring together members of Oxford University who, after a brawl in 1238, had left Oxford and settled elsewhere. This affair, which was fully reported by Matthew Paris, the historian of Henry III's reign, was a serious matter, involving the death of the brother of the Papal Legate. Among those arrested was a student named John de Bridport, another man who had gone from the town to the University.

Giles opened his College (the first university college in England) in the year 1260. Thus the scattered scholars had been elsewhere for 22 years, a sad state of affairs which Giles hoped to remedy by bringing them back, through his College, into a new relationship with Oxford. But where had the scholars been all this time? This is a long-standing mystery which Bridport may help to solve.

The oldest dated document belonging to the town records that, in the year 1240, there was someone called Vincent, Rector of the Schools (or possibly of the scholars) of Bridport. The use of the plural is intriguing, suggesting a university type of arrangement, of several scholars each with his school. In addition, but only during a relatively short period, there were several in the town with the title 'Master'. There were Master John Ruffus, Master Bartholomew, Master Henry (probably a teacher of law), Master Hamund, Master Robert Gervase and Master John de Bridport. Only the last of these, who was an apothecary, remained in Bridport after about 1260, and the rest presumably joined the staff of Vaux College.

The first Warden of that College was Sir John Holteby, of Allington, and the second, Thomas de Bridport. Moreover, the endowment of the College included property and privileges in Allington, Walditch and Bridport. Altogether there is a strong suggestion that the scattered scholars found their refuge in Bridport and continued their work here, though they were probably too few and covered too narrow a range of studies to constitute a university.

Education in Bridport has a long history. There was a grammar school in 1593, and that is lost, but Miss Gundry's infant school preserved for a time the brewhouse which in the 17th century provided funds for that earlier school. William Bishop, the 18th century poor cobbler of West Street, taught children to read and was given sixpence a week by John Gundry for doing it.

In the borough archives are three taxations of the early 14th century. These were royal 'aids' to meet the costs incurred by Edward II in his military adventures. Local collectors were appointed, and their duty was to assess the value of each man's moveable goods and to demand the prescribed tax. Thus in 1315-6 a tax of one-fifteenth was imposed, and those appointed to assess and collect it were Edward Renaud, William Horne, Peter Prestes and Adam de Larkestoke. These were the leading men of the town, all serving as bailiffs round about that time. They took quite a modest view of their own affluence, assessing themselves for taxes of 20d, 18d, 12d and 16d respectively. The wealthiest man in the town was undoubtedly William Bume, whose goods were valued at £9, and his tax assessed accordingly at 12s.

The items valued were: a horse, 10s; a pig, 2s; sailcoth, girth-webs, twine, 40s; rope, flax and hemp, 40s; 2 beds, 10s; brass measures and bowls, 20s; 1 mazer cup, 6s 8d (mazer was a hard wood, usually maple, which could be turned and polished); corn, 20s; a ewer and basin, 4s; a chest and a coffer, 10s; in botels (trusses) of hemp, 17s 4d. There is a large stock of finished goods as well as of raw materials for the twine, net and sailcloth trade, far more than expected to be used and made by one man, even with the help of his family. William Bume is an early instance of an entrepreneur or factor, putting out flax and hemp to cottage workers and receiving from them for re-sale quantities of twine, rope, girth-webbing and sailcloth. (There is, surprisingly, no mention of nets.)

In the second taxation of 1319-20, in which the rate has risen to one twelfth, William Bume is in a different economic position. His horse is now worth only 6s 8d; his jug and basin has declined in value by a shilling, and altogether he is worth only 25s and

8d. However, the assessors are Edward Renaud, Lawrence Elyoth — and William Bume. In the taxation of 1323 his valuation is £3 and his tax at one sixth, 10s. Edward Renaud, no longer an assessor, becomes the town's richest man, with a tax of 26s 8d.

Something seems to have gone wrong after this, for William Bume appears just once as a Bailiff, though he lived until 1349. He was probably a victim of the Black Death. He left a few properties to his son, a niece and a nephew, but all the rest to his daughter, Christine. She too died in 1349 and her will, made after her father's, mentions his bequest to her. Her estate by no means suggests a state of poverty. In money alone she left nearly £11, her servant, Agnes, receiving her best bed, two best robes and £5. All the houses and lands left by her father went to her husband, John Gower, and after him to her son, John Bume. (Note the surname passes through the female side of the family.) The extent of these lands may be judged by the account of a local rate, the Gabella Martini (St Martin's rental) of about 1330. There the name of William Bume appears no less than eleven times, his properties quite widely distributed.

He was certainly a rich man; but his wealth was no defence when the scourge of the Black Death struck the town.

From commoners to King's, for it is not often remembered that Bridport was a royal borough. As Hutchins said, it 'antiently belonged to the crown'. The royal connection goes back at least as far as Alfred the Great, who fortified it. Henry Plantagenet captured it. King John visited it when on hunting trips in Powerstock forest. In those days it ranked as a royal manor, administered by a steward; but it had become an important market town, developing an internal administration of its own, and this was recognised in 1253 by Henry III, who granted a charter and raised the rent. The charter allowed the townsfolk to govern themselves through bailiffs and burgesses and to appoint their own officers. The rent became £16 per annum.

Thenceforth there were many contacts with the crown, some through legislative orders and some by actual visits. Henry IV's second queen, Joan of Navarre, was here early in 1404. His second son, Thomas, Duke of Clarence, was probably the 'Amerall' (Admiral) mentioned as here in June of the same year.

In 1465-6 George, another Duke of Clarence, was in the town, possibly several times and once with Lord Stafford. Were they perhaps plotting here against the Duke's brother, Edward IV? 'False, fleeting, perjured Clarence' was to die in the Tower in 1478, drowned, it is said, in a barrel of malmsey wine.

Later that century, on 5 November 1483, Richard III passed through the town on his way to deal with trouble at Exeter, but stopped only long enough for a drink.

A picture in the Town Hall suggests that Henry VIII came to the town, but this appears to be just a fancy of the painter, Francis Newberry, who was indicating that King's interest in the rope trade.

The most famous visit was that of Prince Charles, after the battle of Worcester in 1651. According to some he was already King Charles II, but the Bridport authorities being Parliamentarians, did not acknowledge his sovereignty until 1660, the year of his accession to the throne. The story goes that on 23 September 1651, Charles passed through the town and decided to stop for a meal at a local inn. There is a contemporary reference to the Red Lion, but the general opinion and the established tradition is that it was the George, a fact proclaimed on the shop front built by Giles Roberts in 1804. Suspecting that he had been recognised, Charles left hurriedly, and escaped his pursuers by dodging down a side-lane, alleged to be Lee Lane, where a stone records the incident.

In more recent times the late King George VI was briefly here during the last war, and his daughter Princess Margaret came to attend the celebrations of the seventh centenary of the granting of the first royal charter in 1253.

That charter was several times confirmed, occasionally with a revision of its terms — by Richard II, Henry VII, Edward VI, Elizabeth I, James I, Charles II and James II. In addition Elizabeth I made a grant of fairs and markets in 1594 in order to compensate the town for the silting-up of its harbour.

The status of the borough changed in 1800, when the government, faced with debt on account of war with France, offered to sell the freehold of the town to the corporation. The offer was accepted and Bridport ceased to be a royal manor and borough. It was still a parliamentary borough, with two members, but even that position was eventually lost. Now, thanks to local government reorganisation, it is no longer even a borough, but a parish, though by courtesy it may call itself a town and appoint a mayor.

One man who deserves some remembrance, though in danger of being forgotten, was Thomas Clarke, the Town Missionary. The title may seem strange, but it reflects a phenomenon of the 19th century. In spite of John Wesley's work in the previous century, industrialisation and the movement into towns had given rise to a population which was outside the normal orbit of the churches — the urban poor. Charles Dickens had much to tell us about them; they existed not just in London, but also in small towns like Bridport. To meet the situation various experiments in down-town mission work were made, sometimes called 'domestic' missions because they were based upon home rather than upon churches and halls.

Thomas Clarke, born in 1818, came of Cheshire farming stock, but began his working life in a Macclesfield silk mill. At the same time he was an enthusiastic young helper of the vicar of Sutton, Macclesfield, Rev Dr Burnett, and when the latter moved to Bradford, Yorks, in 1847, he went with him as a lay worker with the Church Pastoral Aid Society. Unfortunately, after an association of 26 years, there was a serious disagreement between the two men, apparently because Clarke held more extreme Protestant views than Burnett. He therefore moved to Northampton in 1859 to work with the Country Towns Mission.

A few years later, in December 1861, he was invited to Bridport to work from the next month for the Town Mission which had been founded in 1858 by the Rector, Rev Melville Lee. Mr Clarke's work is fully recorded in the annual reports, several of which are still extant and give statistical analyses of the Missionary's activities.

Thus in 1873 we have this list:

'Number of hours employed		1954
,,	meetings held	168
,,	persons addressed at the said meetings	3346
,,	visits, exclusive of those to the sick	3505
,,	visits to the sick and infirm	763
,,	persons addressed while visiting — men, 2,123; women, 4,819; total	6942
,,	times the Scriptures read	3231
,,	Tracts distributed	2520
,,	religious serials — "Cottager", "Friendly Visitor", "Biblical Treasury", "Home Words", "Sunday at Home", sold	1104
,,	persons induced to attend public worship	16
,,	persons induced to unite with Christian Churches	3
,,	children sent to Sunday School	12
,,	drunkards reclaimed	8
,,	hopeful conversions	15
,,	persons relieved and supplied with clothing	160'

The work of the Society was supported by personal subscriptions and by collections at several churches, considerable support coming from evangelical nonconformists. However, the reports show a steadily dwindling income from these sources and increasing difficulty in paying the Missionary. So, when Mr Clarke died in 1893, the work of the Town Mission was wound up.

An almost legendary citizen of Bridport was Giles Roberts, the doctor and apothecary whose shop-front, built for him in 1804, is still a feature of the town-centre. Although it is claimed that he was established in East Street in 1788, records show that he was in West Street, first to the west of the present Post Office and then, from 1799, to the east of it, this being the former home of another doctor, Simon Robinson.

His best-known product was the ointment, *The Poor Man's Friend,* which seemed to be capable of curing almost any skin trouble, from corns to the King's Evil, and which seems to have travelled all over the world. Unfortunately, in spite of its virtues, it could not now be sold, containing as is does the oxides of lead and mercury. But its sale was then supported by numerous unsolicited testimonials, a feature of Robert's public relations. They appeared quite early in the *Sherborne Mercury,* and later in the booklets which he published, sometimes called *The Annual Mentor or Cottager's Companion,* or *Sentimental and Humorous Essays, conducive to Economy, Health and Happiness.* These included short lectures on such themes as sloth or drunkenness and collections of pithy maxims. Also there were pages of letters from grateful users of his ointment and his *Pilulae Antiscrophulae.*

Another feature of his practice was the opening of his surgery on Mondays for giving free advice to the poor, though 'The usual Fee will be expected from persons of ability'.

Dr Roberts is known to have been a Wesleyan and to have been mainly responsible for establishing the Methodist church in the town. There is, however, evidence to suggest that he had earlier been a Dissenter and more radical in his politics than he later became.

He died in 1834 and is buried in St Mary's churchyard. The business passed to his apprentices, Beach and Barnicott, who continued to produce the wonderful ointment. Indeed it was made by Beach & Co until as recently as 1965, and requests for it are still occasionally received from distant parts of the world.

While history is about people, and a town is a community of people, most of them have no memorial, but the occasional photograph may bring them back. Even then they may be nameless, though their picture may tell us something of their period. Pictures of a few former residents of the town and district, have survived more by good fortune than by intent.

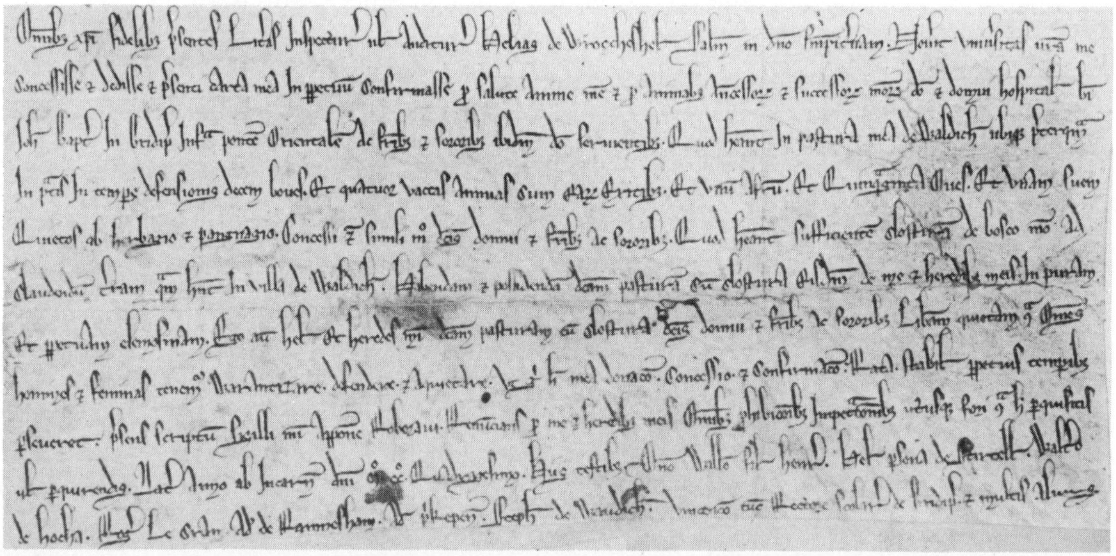

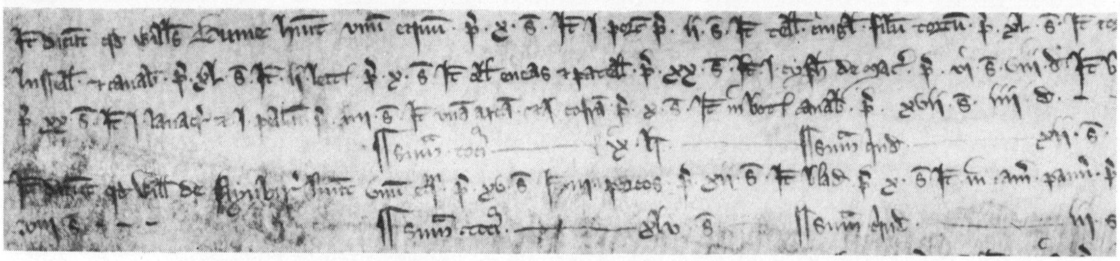

ABOVE: Bridport's oldest dated document. One or two may be older, but this is clearly dated 1240 (m.cc.Quadragesimo). It is a grant of rights of pasture in Walditch to the Hospital of St John the Baptist. It is interesting because the last named witness is Vincent, Rector of the Schools (or scholars) of Bridport. (NR/B3/CD78) BELOW: Part of the taxation of a fifteenth, 1315-6, showing William Bume's assessment. (NR/B3/M35)

ABOVE LEFT: Thomas Clarke, the town missionary. (Rees, London) RIGHT: *The Man of Law's Book:* BELOW: Thomas Clarke and his parish school young men's class in a specially posed photograph on his departure from Bradford (Yorks), 1859. (Mr Booth of Darley Street)

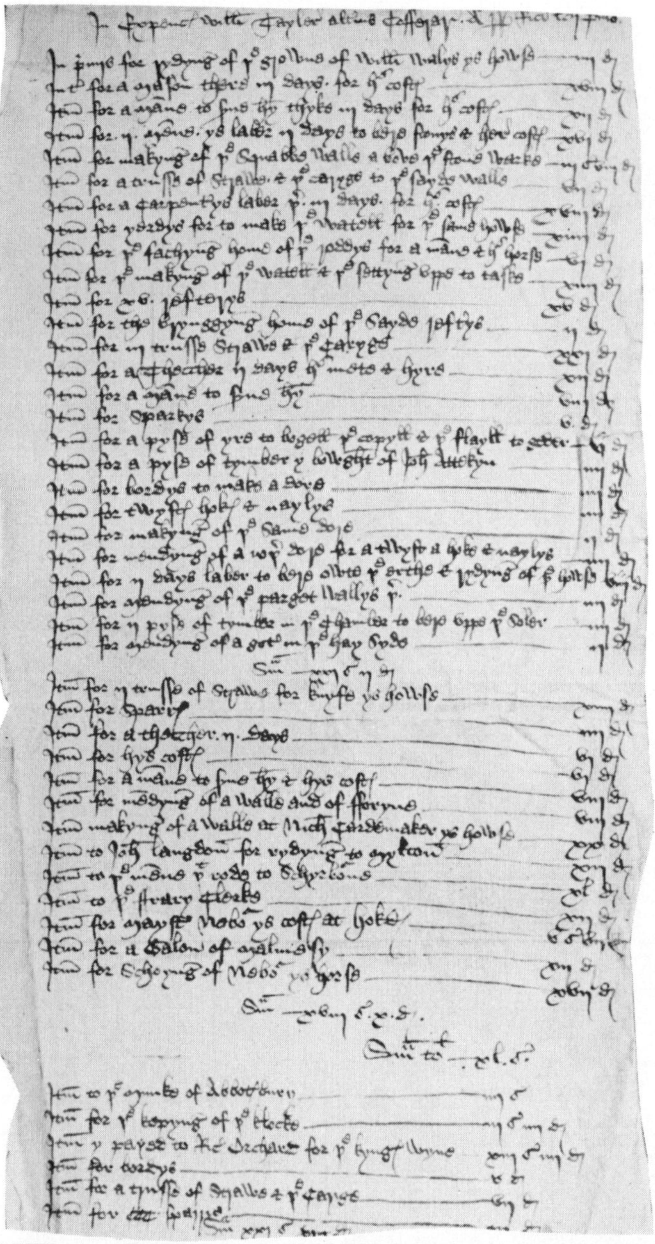

LEFT: A cofferer's account for 1483. A fascinating account by William Taylor, one of the borough treasurers. An intriguing entry reads: 'Item y payed Ric(hard) Orchard for ye King's Wyne xiijs iiijd'. Richard III passed through Bridport on 5 November, 1483. It looks as though he called at Richard Orchard's inn with his troop as he was on his way to Exeter. The sum mentioned looks more like compensation than the actual cost, 13s 4d being exactly one mark. (NR/B3/M6) ABOVE RIGHT: Edward VI on his confirmation (1550) of Henry III's charter of 1253. CENTRE: Queen Elizabeth, on her grant of fairs and markets, 1594. (NR/B3/03 BELOW: Charles II, on his confirmation of ancient rights and liberties, 1666. (NR/B3/K8)

LEFT: The stone which commemorates the story of a famous escape. (BM) RIGHT: James II's confirmation, 1686. (NR/B3/K9) BELOW: The corporation celebrates Queen Victoria's Jubilee, 1897. (BM)

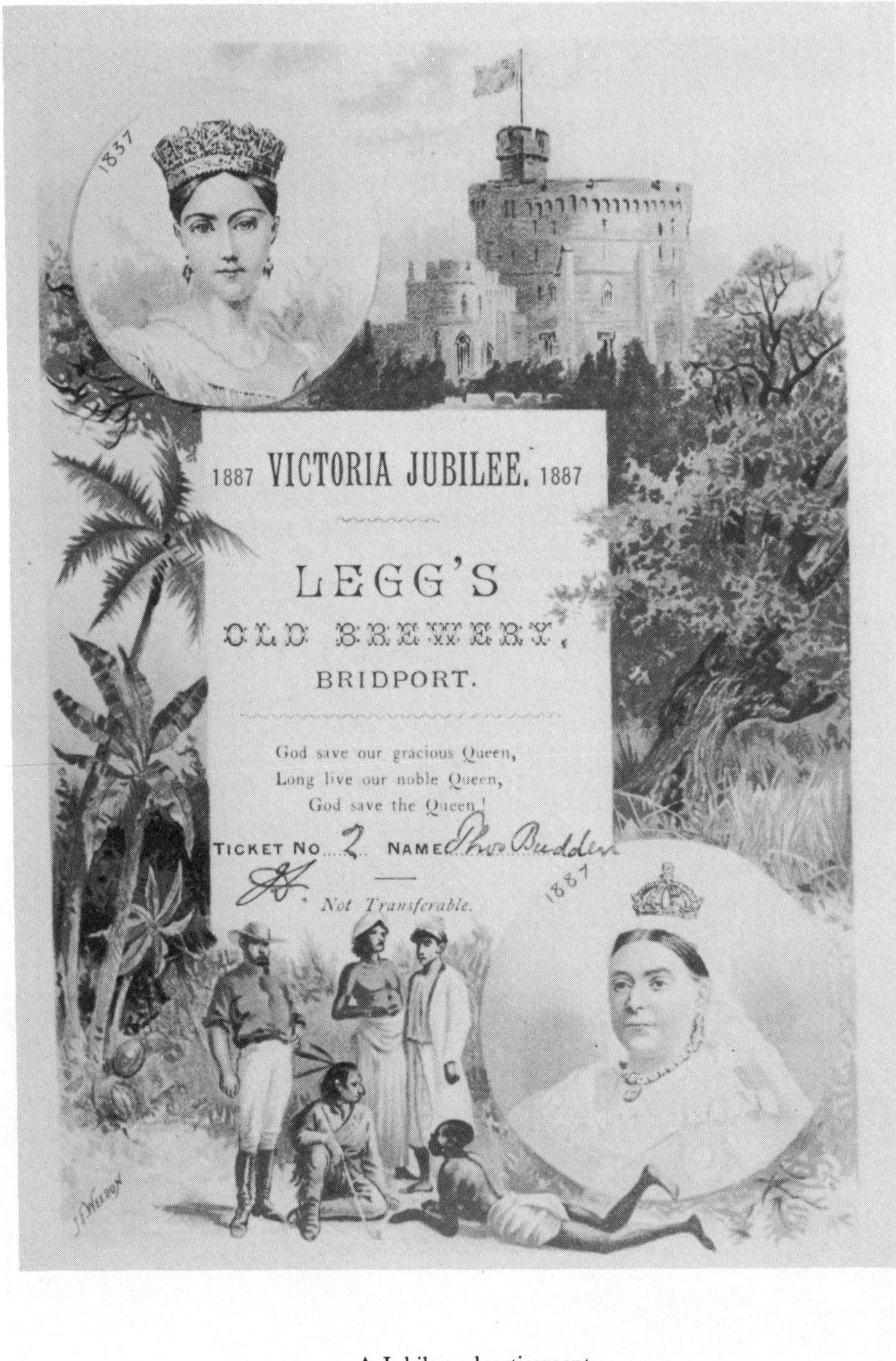

A Jubilee advertisement.

ABOVE: Celebrating Edward VII's coronation, 1902. (BM) LEFT: George V's coronation, 1911. (BM) RIGHT: Proclamation of Queen Elizabeth II, 1953. (BM)

ABOVE: Princess Margaret at the Pageant to celebrate the 700th anniversary of Henry III's charter of 1253. (BM) BELOW: The Town Council of Bridport Borough, 1968, Ald Miss F. M. Reynolds, Mayor. (BM) Left to right, back row; M. J. Fearn, S. A. Turner, J.C. Angus PHI, L. H. Dibdin, J. W. McCarthy, C. J. Pemberton, P. C. Jeaves, F. M. Watts BS, J. V. Payne BT. Middle row; V. S. C. Keech, A. Cummins, R. I. Forbes, Mrs K. M. Shirley, F. B. Chubb, E. Lewis, A. Baines, F. Lines JP, L. A. J. Radnar. Front row; Ald H. Lewis, Ald H. G. Smith, Canon J. P. Hinton, A. B. Mason, F. M. Reynolds, Eliot Andrews, Ald S. Gale MBE, Ald W. J. Spenser, Ald P. C. Norfolk. Mace Bearers; J. Tattershall, L. A. Follett.

ABOVE: The last Rural District Council, 1974, A. A. J. Palmer Esq, Chairman. (BM) Left to right, back row; E. Andrews (clerk), E. G. Fry, D. Burdon, J. G. Willy, C. W. B. Lucas, Miss E. M. Bickford, Gp Capt F. L. Newall, S. J. Norman, Miss I. M. C. Caddy, R. E. A. Foulgar, V. L. A. Seller (dep clerk) Col H. Cantan, W. H. Woodward, E. G. Yates (surveyor), R. Wood, J. C. Angus (PHI). Front row; Maj E. Golding, H. M. Latto, F. H. White, Lt Col H. J. G. Weld, A. A. J. Palmer (chairman), H. Williams, Mrs M. E. Densham-Smith, Miss A. G. Mackenzie (dep tre), O. A. Aburrow, Dr E. E. Hodgson (MOH), J. R. Newman (dep PHI). Absent: A. B. Mason, W. McLellan. CENTRE: A Beating of Bounds, probably 1926. (BM) BELOW: Laying the foundation stone of the Allington flats, 1947, Alderman F. S. Cornick, Mayor. (PS/BM)

ABOVE: One of the hazards of public service, 1891. (NR/BM) BELOW: Three studies of Bessie Turner (Mrs Bessie Clarke) who became the daughter-in-law of Thomas Clarke, the town missionary, and mother of 'Miss Gertie', a well-loved local teacher: LEFT: at 16 years old, 1883, (Barrett & Co) CENTRE: in her 20s (Wm Barret & Son) and RIGHT: the mature woman. (H.H.Hill)

LEFT: Two Burton Bradstock fisherwomen. (BM) RIGHT: Mr Brownsden, coal merchant, 1893. (T.A. Colfox) BELOW LEFT: A Puncknowle postman, George Kearley. (BM) CENTRE: Samuel Satchwich, of Bothenhampton, chief officer of coastguards. (BM) RIGHT: Gulielma Stephens, 1837-92, a founder of the Literary and Scientific Institute. (BM)

ABOVE LEFT: Miss Harriet Crabb, who lived to be nearly 99, and remembered that she had worn yellow shoes when they celebrated the victory of Waterloo. RIGHT: Giles Roberts, the Bridport doctor, his famous ointment, and a sample of his good advice. (MT/BM/E.A.Blakey) BELOW LEFT: The Crabb sisters, Miss Harriet, Mrs Brownsdon and her husband, and Mrs Peter Brown.

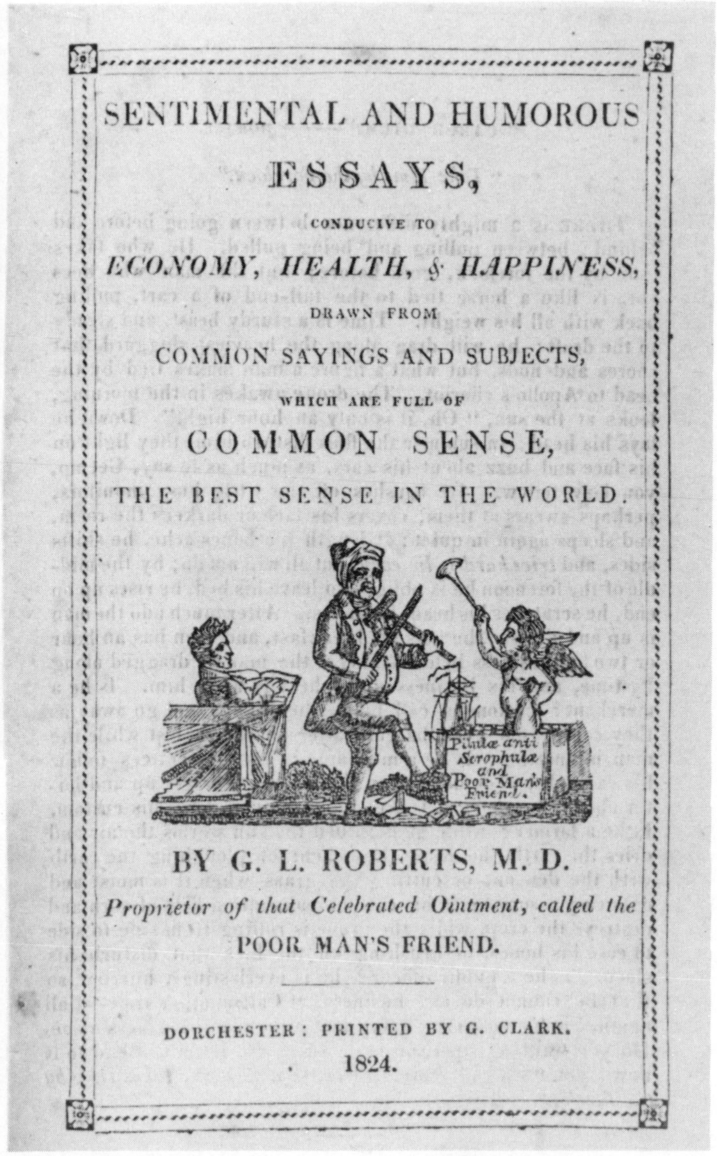

SENTIMENTAL AND HUMOROUS

ESSAYS,

CONDUCIVE TO

ECONOMY, HEALTH, & HAPPINESS,

DRAWN FROM

COMMON SAYINGS AND SUBJECTS,

WHICH ARE FULL OF

COMMON SENSE,

THE BEST SENSE IN THE WORLD.

BY G. L. ROBERTS, M. D.

Proprietor of that Celebrated Ointment, called the

POOR MAN'S FRIEND.

DORCHESTER: PRINTED BY G. CLARK.

1824.

ABOVE: The shop in East Street which Giles Roberts opened in 1805, on the site of the former George Inn. (BM) BELOW: The memorial to Giles Roberts in the parish church burial ground. (PEP/BM) LEFT: The General School, King Street, as seen from Crock Lane, 1855.

LEFT: Mrs Adlem, sister-in-law of Mrs Peter Brown and like her of King Street, with her companion, Miss Weightman. RIGHT: George R. Wadham and his wife, formerly Miss Amy Lilian Spiller, at their home in Ceylon, where he was engaged by the Crown Agents as construction engineer for the railway. In this photo, c1909, the children are now Mrs Gladys Buckler, of Shipton Lane, Burton, and George Wadham, of West Allington. Unfortunately their father was drowned in 1918, when the ship in which he was returning on leave was in collision in Liverpool Bay. (Mrs Buckler) BELOW: The Turner family, c1900, including Mrs Bessie Clarke and her four children. The boy on the right is probably Morny Turner, well-known reporter of the *Bridport News*.

ABOVE: The Broadley family of the Knapp, Bradpole, 1901. (W.L. Stephens/BM) BELOW: The Colfox family of Rax House, c1872. Miss Harriet, Miss Alice, her cousin, Thomas and Mrs Louisa Colfox. On the left are the domestic staff. (The late Mrs C.A. Hare)

ABOVE: The family of J. T. Stephens, of Wanderwell. (E.C. Hare/BM)
BELOW: Wedding group: Bertha Rendall to Murray Urquart. (BM)

The children of Major T. A. Colfox, of Coneygar House, c1893; a most appealing picture taken by their father.

TOP LEFT: J. E. Sheppard, for 44 years a guard on the GWR, the last 32 on the Bridport branch. (BM) RIGHT: Jack Hutchings demonstrates a once familiar instrument. (PEP/BM) LEFT: C. R. Kendall, (centre), winner of 1st prize in the 2nd annual potato competition of St Mary's allotments, 1923, digging 119½ lbs from 45 sets.

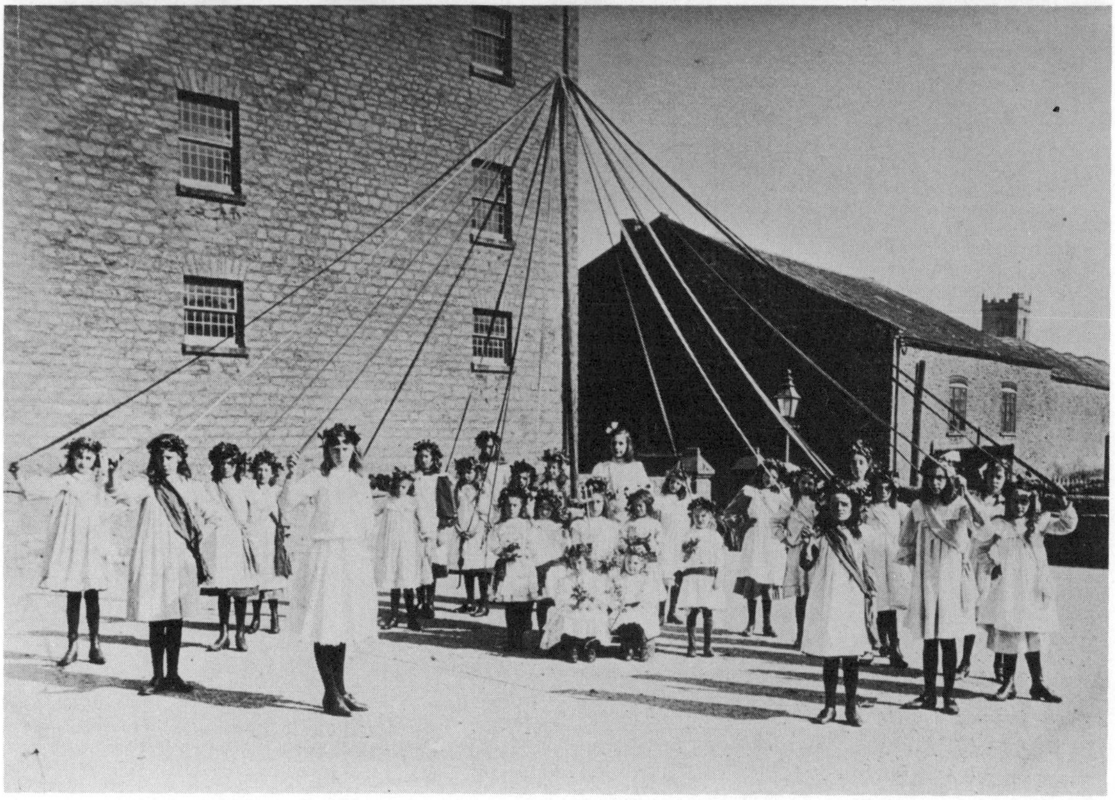

ABOVE: Miss Gundry's Infant School, c1900. (BM) BELOW: Maypole dancing at St Mary's School, Gundry Lane. (BM)

ABOVE: A General School class c1903, with Gertie Clarke fourth from right and Dorothy Spiller extreme right, both middle row. (BM) CENTRE: Another General School class. (BM) BELOW: The girls' teachers of the General School, Miss Brownsdon, head teacher. (BM)

ABOVE: Three teachers at Askerswell School during World War I: Miss Gertie Clark and Miss Dorothy Spiller of Bridport, and Miss Dorothy Kennett (front) of Symondsbury. BELOW: A class at Miss Gundry's. (BM)

ABOVE: West Bay on a Whitsun holiday c1870. (BM) BELOW: Detail from last picture, enlarged to show the shipbuilding yard. (BM)

Harbour and West Bay

Lyme Bay is a dangerous stretch of water, particularly when a spring tide has the backing of a strong south-westerly wind. Then the waves approaching the Chesil beach are most impressive, even terrifying, in their height and reach. When they burst upon Bridport harbour entrance they can do a great deal of damage. Yet this dangerous piece of coast has few places of refuge. Lyme has a harbour, but from there eastwards to Portland there is no security.

It is possible that once there was shelter in the Bridport creek. Borings taken on the glebe land by St Mary's church suggest that, within the last thousand years, there was an ebb and flow of tidal water right up to the town. It may well be that, prior to a recession of the coast, the Chesil sand did not obstruct the outflow as it certainly did later. Hutchins is probably mistaken in assuming the existence of sluices in the 13th century, his translation of the word 'gurges' having little authority for that period. Yet his assumption has coloured much of the later thinking about Bridport as a port. (The word 'port' may, of course, mean no more than 'market'.) It is quite possible that ships of modest draught, as they would be, came inland on the tide, enabling the town to be, as Queen Elizabeth said, 'a port of great celebrity and resort'.

Unfortunately this did not last, and the recorded history of the port relates largely to the efforts to make a new harbour, though also to legal problems which may have been created by the progressive loss of deep sea access. As early as 1122 there was trouble with the monks of Caen over trespass by Bridport people across their land in Burton. This may have been because of attempts to move sand blown across the outflow by storms. There was more trouble in 1275. It was not until late in the 14th century that a serious effort was made to build a proper harbour. It was not successful, nor was another attempt in the 15th century. The cause of the trouble was the choking of the outlet by Chesil sand. At the end of the 16th century hope was abandoned and Bridport granted the status of an inland market town. There was still occasional talk about trying to reinstate the harbour, but nothing effective was done.

Early in the 18th century new efforts were made to obtain legislation and in 1721 an Act of Parliament was passed; 20 years later a harbour and piers were built. The sand was still a problem, but eventually the scheme was adopted, and is still used, of 'scouring' the harbour by holding back the river behind sluices before releasing it at the best time for flushing away the sand.

Trade began to increase from about this time and reached its peak around the middle of the 19th century. Sailcloth, lines and nets were the main exports, and also local butter and cheese. The main imports were hemp, flax, timber, coal and a variety of general goods. There was also some ship-building activity to the west of the harbour. Nicholas Bools was building ships towards the end of the 18th century; John Cox, and then his son, Elias, in the 19th.

The area around the harbour was included in the new borough boundaries in 1835, and was then known as Bridport Harbour. But when the railway came in 1884, the name given to the station, perhaps with an eye to tourism, was West Bay, by which the locality has since been known.

Fishing has always been an activity associated with the harbour, and mackerel, sprats and other fish, are still brought in. Sea-going trade, however, has much declined, though in recent years it has been possible to see the occasional load of Baltic timber landed. Mainly the area is devoted to holiday-making. The opening of the railway stimulated residential development, and the closing of the railway did not bring it to an end. The giant block of flats, Pier Terrace (otherwise Noah's Ark), on the east, is now matched by holiday flats and a shopping precinct on the west, where the shipyard used to be. (Ship-building has been revived, but near the town, where Newbridge Boats build luxury yachts.) A pioneer municipal camp-site flourishes where once salt was extracted. The east cliff has a golf course, the west cliff a suburban development. And though it cannot rival other West Country resorts, West Bay has bingo and candy floss, a regatta week and an esplanade, this last the gift of Thomas Colfox and opened in 1887 as part of the Jubilee celebrations.

The esplanade and the harbour piers sometimes suffer severely from gales and high seas, and occasionally the sea breaks through, flooding the plain towards the town. But, come summer and after the necessary repairs, the sun shines and the holiday makers come back.

Perhaps the railway had the right idea. West Bay is much more appropriate than Bridport Harbour.

After the closure of the shipyard these holiday chalets were built.

ABOVE: A view from the East Cliff, c1890. (BM) CENTRE: The east side of the harbour, showing Pier Terrace and the Bridport Arms. (BM) BELOW: Heavy seas make the entrance hazardous. (BM)

ABOVE: Sailing vessels berthed in the harbour. (BM) BELOW: Unloading. (BM)

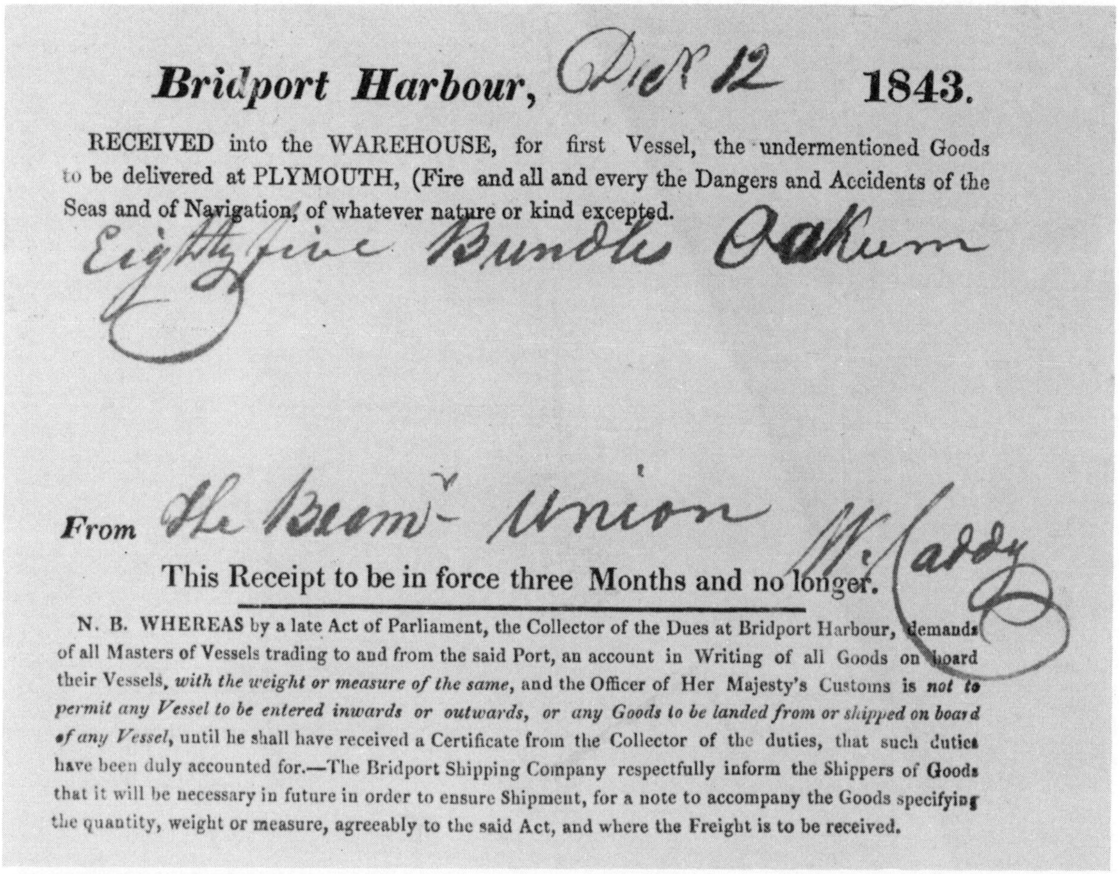

Bridport Harbour, Decr 12 **1843.**

RECEIVED into the WAREHOUSE, for first Vessel, the undermentioned Goods to be delivered at PLYMOUTH, (Fire and all and every the Dangers and Accidents of the Seas and of Navigation, of whatever nature or kind excepted.

Eighty five Bundles Oakum

From the Beam^r Union W. Caddy

This Receipt to be in force three Months and no longer.

N. B. WHEREAS by a late Act of Parliament, the Collector of the Dues at Bridport Harbour, demands of all Masters of Vessels trading to and from the said Port, an account in Writing of all Goods on board their Vessels, *with the weight or measure of the same*, and the Officer of Her Majesty's Customs is ***not to permit any Vessel to be entered inwards or outwards, or any Goods to be landed from or shipped on board of any Vessel***, until he shall have received a Certificate from the Collector of the duties, that such duties have been duly accounted for.—The Bridport Shipping Company respectfully inform the Shippers of Goods that it will be necessary in future in order to ensure Shipment, for a note to accompany the Goods specifying the quantity, weight or measure, agreeably to the said Act, and where the Freight is to be received.

ABOVE: Receipt for harbour dues. (And guess what they had been doing at the workhouse!) (BM) BELOW: Hemp from Riga. (BM)

ABOVE: Coal from .... South Wales? (BM) RIGHT: High tide and rough water. (BM) CENTRE: Waves pounding the Mound, which was recently washed away. (BM) BELOW: Gravel is a valuable local commodity, exported to many parts of the world. (BM) INSET: Mr Good's warehouse with assorted grades of sand and gravel. (BM)

ABOVE: Holiday makers early this century. (BM) CENTRE: Off to Weymouth on the paddle-steamer, *Victoria.* (BM) BELOW: The harbour as a beauty spot. (BM)

More recent holidays in tent and caravan: an aerial view of West Bay. (BM)

ENDPAPERS — FRONT: Map of Bridport from Hutchins' *History and Topography of the County of Dorset,* 1774. BACK: Bridport seal; the second oldest design. (NR/B3/PQ34)

Bibliography

Bayley, A. R.	*The Great Civil War in Dorset,* Barnicott & Pearce, 1910
Beckles, G.	*The Bridport Story,* Bridport Industries Ltd, 1953
Benfield, E.	*Dorest (The County Book Series)* R. Hale Ltd, 1950
Bettey, J. H.	*Dorset (City and County History Series)* David & Charles, 1974
Broadley, A. M.	*The Royal Miracle,* Stanley Paul, 1912
Colfox, E. H. & C.A.(ed)	*The Colfox Family Papers*
Douch, R.	*A Handbook of Local History: Dorset,* University of Bristol, 1952
Jackson, B. L. & Tattershall, M. J.	*The Bridport Branch,* Oxford Publishing Company, 1976
Fletcher, J. M. J.	*Bishop Giles of Bridport* and *De Vaux College,* 1934
Gardiner, D.	*Companion into Dorset,* Methuen, 1949
Good, R	*The Lost Villages of Dorset,* Dovecote Press, 1979
Heath, F. R.	*Dorset (The Little Guide Series),* Methuen 1949
Horsfall, M.	*Life in Bridport, 1898-1918,* Toucan Press, 1969
Hutchins, J.	*History and Topography of the County of Dorset,* 1774
Kerr, B.	*Bound to the Soil,* John Baker, 1968
Leland, J. (ed L. T. Smith)	*Itinerary in England and Wales,* Centaur Press, 1964
Maskell, J.	*History and Topography of Bridport,* Frost, 1855
Matthews, A. W.	*The Story of West Bay,* privately printed, 1901
Mee, A. (ed)	*Dorset (King's England),* Hodder, 1967
Pevsner, N. & Newman	*The Buildings of Dorset,* Penguin Books, 1972
Pitt-Rivers, M.	*Dorset (Shell Guides),* Faber, 1966
Rowson, J. W.	*Bridport in the Great War,* Laurie, 1923
Scroggs, E. S.	*A Brief Guide to the Municipal Records,* Bridport Bor, 1953
Sellman, R. R.	*Illustrations of Dorset History,* Methuen, 1960
Short, E. B.	*A Respectable Society: 1593-1835,* Moonraker, 1976
Short, J. L.	*Lecture on Mortality and Health,* Prince, 1849
Taylor, C.	*Dorset (The Making of the English Landscape),* Hodder & Stoughton, 1970
Treves, F.	*Dorset (Highways and Byways Series)*
Udal, J. S.	*Dorsetshire Folk Lore,* Toucan Press, 1970
Wainwright, T.	*The Bridport Borough Records and MSS,* Bridport News, 1900
Weinstock, M.	*Old Dorset,* David and Charles, 1967
Weinstock, M.	*More Dorset Studies,* Longmans, Dorchester, 1960
Wood-Legh, K. L.	*A Small Household in the 15th Century,* Manchester University Press

Royal Commission on Historical Monuments: West Dorset Report, HMSO, 1952
Royal Commission on Historical Manuscripts: Sixth Report and Appendix, HMSO, 1877
The Victoria County History: Dorset, ed W. Page, Archibald, Constable, 1908
Proceedings of the Dorset Natural History and Archaeological Society
The Dorset Year Book
Notes and Queries for Somerset and Dorset
Various *Directories* and *Almanacs*
County Guides: Ward-Locke, Geographia, Penguin, etc and *Black's Guide to Dorset,* 1866
Official Guides to Bridport and District

Index

Numbers in *italics* refer to illustrations

Subscribers

Presentation Copies

1 Bridport Town Council
2 West Dorset District Council
3 Dorset County Council
4 Bridport Library
5 Bridport Museum
6 Sir John Colfox
7 Miss Frances Reynolds

8 Basil Short
9 John Sales
10 Clive & Carolyn Birch
11 Mrs P. J. Roper
12 Mrs S. Stalley
13 J. Millest
14 Mrs C. B. Gallafent
15 Mr & Mrs R.G. Marriott
16 Miss C. G. Kenway
17 Miss S. A. Brown
18 Miss M. Treadwell
19 Lynn Horniblow
20 Mrs Doreen Barwick
21 Miss Marjorie Serpell
22 E. Stevens
23 Mrs Rosemary Caddy
24 Miss E. Newman
25 Miss A. H. Tett
26 A. E. Wrixton
27 C. A. Hodges
28 Mrs Dorothy J. Harrison
29 Mrs J. M. Minns
30 A. G. Lee
31 G. D. Guy
32 Betty Anne Lee
33 Dr H. E. S. Piarin
34 M. J. Coombs
35 A. R. Potts
36 Peter Chard
37 Mrs C. A. Golds
38 Mrs B. M. St John
39 Martin D. Grier
40 C. E. Perkins
41 Mr & Mrs Toogood
42 P. D. Chantler
43 Dr & Mrs Philip H. Cottrill
44 Mrs E. Winder
45 Mrs H. Lee
46 Miss F. M. Reynolds
47 K. J. Giles
48 Mrs C. M. Hann
49 Mrs M. S. Mosley
50 M. L. Wrixton
51 B. R. Brailey
52 Rhowena N. Woodruffe
53 Mrs J. Holland
54 G. Skevington
55 Jennifer June Jack
56 Mrs Lois Jaffe
57 58 R. Webster
59 L. G. Nicholson
60 J. Garrett
61 Mrs A. M. Dumbreck
62 Mrs J. R. Dibdin
63 Miss J. Biddlecombe
64 G. G. King
65 W. L. Chapman-Andrews
66 Mr & Mrs F. Jerram
67 J. F. Leggett
68 Mrs A. Firth
69 Henrietta Fuller
70 Mary Cox
71 Robert Knight
72 A. E. Currah
73 Mrs C. O'Shea
74 Mr & Mrs Tom Sharpe
75 C. I. Cook
76 Cmdr G. J. Holt RN (Rtd)
77 Mrs & Mrs D.A. Hann
78 Mrs L. Bartlett
79 Roy Fursman
80 Major R.J. Kidston MBE
81 Mrs Hunkin
82 Miss J. Turner
83 R. W. Ludgate
84 Mr & Mrs K. Crossley
85 Mrs D. Lyall
86 Anne Traves
87 B. W. Culpin
88 M. E. Currah
89 L. W. Croad
90 Mrs Fiona M. Tolley
91 T. P. Harrison
92 Richmond Minto
93 A. J. Hutchings
94 R.F. & S.C. Williams
95 G. Burroughs
96 Mrs P. M. Linlard
97 Mr & Mrs B. Kinchin
98 Mr & Mrs G.W.A. Matthews
99 Canon Geoffrey Goodall
100 Mrs K. L. Sealey
101 P. Nicolayson
102 R. E. Hill
103 J. Wood
104 106 D. J. Gill
107 Miss E. Fox
108 Mrs J. Prince
109 110 Mr & Mrs Harsinger
111 Brian Hann
112 Mr & Mrs V. Seaton
113 Mrs A. C. Quarmby
114 H. Henry
115 Miss N. A. Henry
116 Mrs D. P. Read
117 Mr & Mrs Goodwin
118 Mr & Mrs F. Dransfield
119 Michael Tattershall
120 Martin Lovelace
121 Mr & Mrs Ronald Frampton
122 Miss J. Dunn
123 David Ball
124 Reginald Croker
125 126 Miss D. Wood
127 Town Clerk
128 G. Y. Strawson
129 Mrs J. Walbrin
130 Miss Daisy Boxall & Miss K. Vernall
131 Rev N. Skinner
132 Mr & Mrs J. Whittaker
133 Miss H. Vernall
134 Rev Martin Bell
135 B. E. F. Doyle
136 F. J. Cooper
137 B. J. Rees
138 J. G. Kirtley
139 P. C. Norfolk
140 Miss M. Alvey Fletcher
141 J. Liversidge
142 Misses, Mr & H.C.M. Jellicoe
143 Mrs M. Ruston
144 Mr & Mrs Malcolm Waterfall
145 Mr K. M. Shirley
146 Miss C. M. Roberts
147 Dr J. H. P. Pafford
148 St Catherine's School
149 Miss D. Sweet
150 Miss D. M. Cross
151 Mrs Fay Cox
152 Mrs E. Winder
153 Miss D. Smeaton
154 Mr & Mrs R. Hindson
155 R. J. Warren
156 Mrs N. B. Davies
157 Mrs M.D.E.G. Eedle
158 J. I. Parkes
159 Mrs E. Stearn
160 Jacqueline Taylor
161 P. C. Day
162 A. H. Hart
163 Mrs G. A. de Cenl
164 Mrs H. John
165 E. Farmer
166 P. J. Garland
167 A. E. Sweet
168 D. Rockett
169 K. C. Fudge
170 C. Robin Upton
171 D. A. Greening
172 Mrs J. Russ
173 Mrs A. Huxter
174 Bridport W I
175 Dr T. Hedley White
176 Mrs E. M. Barber
177 Mrs Susan Stalley
178 L. Payne-Gill
179 A. E. Watson
180 Mr & Mrs J. A. Stedman
181 G. D. Pursall
182 Sam Dunn
183 Gail White
184 M. E. Spacagna
185 Mr & Mrs L. P. Burse
186 F. J. Watson
187 G. C. Good
188 R. Harvey
189 S. J. Wimhurst
190 N. M. Shipp
191 Mrs G. H. Line
192 Mrs Nora Andrews
193 K. L. Palk
194 Mrs Enid Cooper
195 Mrs M. H. Cripps
196 Miss Z. K. Johnson
197 Mrs V. E. A. Clifford
198 E. Tunnicliff
199 Mrs J. E. Andrews
200 Miss J. Stanley
201 Mrs E. A. Green
202 Miss Bridget Eveleigh
203 George Crawshaw
204 Mrs B. J. M. Commer
205 Miss Edwards
206 F. P. Gough
207 J. Wallis
208 D. Hounsell
209 P. Pearce
210 Mrs Christobel Moullin
211 Mrs H. B. Roach
212 J. C.H. Templer
213 R. G. W. Holding
214 M. Pinkett
215 Mrs J. Anderson
216 R. G. Doran
217 Miss B. P. Lawrence
218 J. R. G. Fuszard
219 Miss E. I. Randall-Jones
220 C. V. Gentle
221 R. T. Golding
222 Mrs S. Secton-Smith
223 A. P. Brooker
224 Mrs John Baic
225 E. L. Brockman
226 Mrs D. L. Williams
227 A. J. Warren
228 Mrs R. A. Hedges
229 R. L. Powell
230 Mrs E. G. Tritton
231 Mr W. P. Glover & Miss P. P. Glover

232 P. A. E. Davis
233 David & Liba Short
234 John & Susan Palfreyman
235 Martin Short
236 Thomas Williams
237 Joan D. Grundell
238 D. E. Ackerman
239 Miss R. Freeman Smith
240 Dr C. J. Wrigley
241 J. Edwards
242 G. Davies
243 Mrs S. Stoodley
244 Mrs G. W. Payne
245 Mrs B. G. Walker
246 Mrs C. A. Collings
247 A. G. Munden
248 Dr Harold C. Gough
249 W. C. E. Saunders
250 F. J. S. Phillips
251 Mrs W. Payne
252 Miss A. Salt
253 Mrs A. Paul
254 Mr & Mrs R. J. Barrett
255 R. Moody
256 Mrs G. L. M. Buckler
257 Miss E. Yates
258 T. Henley-Coulson
259 Mrs J. Swaffield
260 Mr & Mrs A. E. Fisder
261 Diana Hawley
262 Ralph Mansell
263 Mrs V. Elliott
264 Stephen Finch
265 Mrs J. Walton
266 J. B. Threlfall
267 R. Gartland
268 Mrs G. Shaw
269 Capt F. Townsend
270 Mrs E. M. Kendall
271 Peter Dodsworth
272 Mr & Mrs L. F. Starkey
273 Mrs S. Weaver
274 Mrs S. Huxter
275 Gerald Gibbons
276 Vaughan Robbins
277 Mr & Mrs T. Kearley
278 Mrs P. Nicolayson
279 Mrs Lorna Sealey
280 A. F. T. Brown
281 Mrs E. B. Wild
282 Mr & Mrs M.E. Farmer
283 G. V. Steer
284 Miss H. Minter
285 D. W. M. Barnikel
286 Alan & Maura Page
287 H. Wright
288 W. H. Balson
289 Mr & Mrs L. Furminger
290 Mrs N. Sebright
291 Mr & Mrs Alan Wilkinson
292 J. Shackleton
293 Mr & Mrs D.G. Symes
294 J. Stevens Cox
295 Eric Dunford
296 Laurence Hallett
297 R. Bramble
298 Miss J. M. Sellers
299 Visitation Convent
300 Mrs N. Hibbard
301 M. Guyer
302 S. Eveleigh
303 M. B. Yates
304 A. E. C. Wylde
305 Mrs S. Chester
306 M. Farmer
307 A. E. Beaven
308 Ms Gregg-Smith
309 R. Smith
310 D. England
311 Miss D. S. Edwards
312 Miss A. M. Edwards
313 E. C. Forsey
314 Mrs S. Lawrence
315 C. P. Fox
316 Mrs F. Follett
317 J. W. Capel
318 Mr & Mrs C. D. Vallance
319 Mrs V. Roberts
320 Desmond Bye
321 S. C. Goodwin
322 C. G. Smith
323 Geoffrey Foot
324 Mrs M. Scott
325 Mrs E. M. Barber
326 Miss E. Sykes
327 Miss P.M.L. Hughes
328 Flt Lt E. Jenner
329 M. Cross
330 Stephen Smith
331 M. J. Sutton
332 D. E. A. Flynn
333 Mrs Audrey Ford
334 Mrs A. E. Skerry
335 Mrs H. I. Jesty
336 P. H. Loving
337 Mr & Mrs W.A. Read
338 Mr & Mrs R.F. Read
339 Mrs Nancy Richards
340 Robert B. Conway
341 Miss F. Nicholson
342 R. E. Banfield
343 Miss N. C. Garland
344 Joan & Isabel M. Rendell
345, 346 Sylvia Pitcher
347 Richard D. Mabb
348, 349 Major J.S. Bartholomew
350 Mrs D. J. Payne
351 Mareery Livesey
352 Miss A.C. Mackenzie
353 B. W. Tall
354 Suzanne Barter
355 Simon Barter
356 Ivor C. Caddy
357 Elsa Taylor
358 Anthony J. Toulman
359 Katherine Barker
360 Hilda M. R. Gudge
361 Audrey J. Bailey
362 Edna Handel
363 F. J. Pugsley
364 Elizabeth O. Cockburn
365, 366 Mrs R. H. Hillier
367 Ben Cox
368 Mr & Mrs Wessel
369 E. D. Gazeley
370 Alban Wylde
371, 372 Stanley E. Kemp
373 Peter & Olive Woodward
374 Arthur Pearse
375 Justin S. Mallinson
376 Diana Davis
377 P. S. Bryant
378 J. Wreford
379 Mrs Joan Gent
380 I. Williams
381 Sandra Mae Bowles
382 J. Hawkins
383, 384 H.F.V. Johnstone
385, 387 Miss F. M. Reynolds
388 Mrs T. W. Best
389 Colfox Comp School
390 C. T. Samwaye
391 J. H. Dossor
392 R. S. Johnson
393 Olivia Hole OBE
394 Miss E. M. Yonge
395 N. G. G. Townsend
396 Mrs N. Warren
397 R. A. Skevington
398 Charles Rockett
399 W. T. G. Perrott
400 R. S. A. Johnson
401, 402 F. W. Townsend
403 E. P. Jordan
404 D. E. Joyce
405 J.C. &. R.N. Palmer Ltd
406 St Mary's Primary School
407 Mrs S. Pearce
408 F. M. &. J. Shipway
409 R. Richards
410 Mrs C. E. Desborough
411 M. J. Ridler
412, 413 H. G. Whitfield
414 David Wyatt
415 J. R. Newman
416 Mrs V. Sherrington
417 Miss W. A. Cox
418 H. L. Hix
419 Miss Deborah Gillingham
420 Dr J. W. Woodhead
421 Mrs I. E. Drew
422 Sister Superior, Visitation Convent
423 H. C. Bartlett
424 Mrs D. M. Giacomini
425 Mrs E. Dunsby
426 Keith Alner
427, 428 Ivan Clark
429 Mrs A. L. Bale
430 G. Waggett
431 Mahala Alice Harding
432 J. C. Boldro
433 Harry S. F. Rowsell
434 Miss J. J. Bollins
435 Miss E. O. Jordan
436 G. F. Walker
437 Miss P. F. Norris-Jones
438 E. M. Brown
439 Miss J. M. Hall
440 Fred James
441, 443 Mrs R. Parfitt
444 George C. Morrison
445 Mrs J. E. Tighe
446 Mary Jennifer Shllaker
447 Mr & Mrs P. F. Bailey
448 Brian Adlam
449 Mrs C. M. Coward
450 Frederick John Scaddine
451 R. H. Meech
452 E. J. D. Balson
453 Robert J. Garrett
454, 455 A. Wrieley
456 J. M. Parker
457 Mrs H. Thomson
458, 475 Dorset County Library
476 Mrs J. Pasmore
477 Mrs Andrew Lobb
478 Mrs V. Pooley
479 D. G. Bulpit
480 B. G. M. Beaumont
481 Mrs P. M. Davis
482 Mrs B. G. Joy
483 M. Tuck
484 E. Silvester
485 J. Altham
486, 487 Mrs Buckler
488 Mrs W. Mitchell
489 Mrs B. Webber
490 George Haybittle
491 Beverley Marshall
492 Miss P. E. Gale
493 Miss C. Preece
494 G. Coombs
495 Miss E. Coombs
496 Mrs Holloway
497 Dr I. H. Griffiths
498 Derek Cash
499 Jennifer Best
500 Mrs M. Poole
501 Mrs L. T. Haynes
502 Andrew Bell
503 R. J. Barraclough